TWINS

TWINS

First Edition.
Copyright © Hoxton Mini Press 2018.
All rights reserved.
All photographs © Peter Zelewski.

Introduction by Naomi and Alexandria Hewston.

Design and sequence by Peter Zelewski and Hoxton Mini
Press. With special thanks to Carter Studio for the design
work of *Sisters* by Sophie Harris-Taylor.

A CIP catalogue record for this book is available from the
British Library.

ISBN 978-1-910566-43-5

First published in the United Kingdom in 2018
by Hoxton Mini Press.

To order books, collector's editions and signed prints
please go to: www.hoxtonminipress.com
Printed and bound by Livonia Print, Latvia.

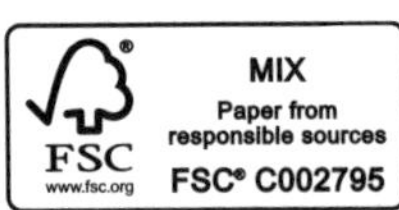

TWINS
Peter Zelewski

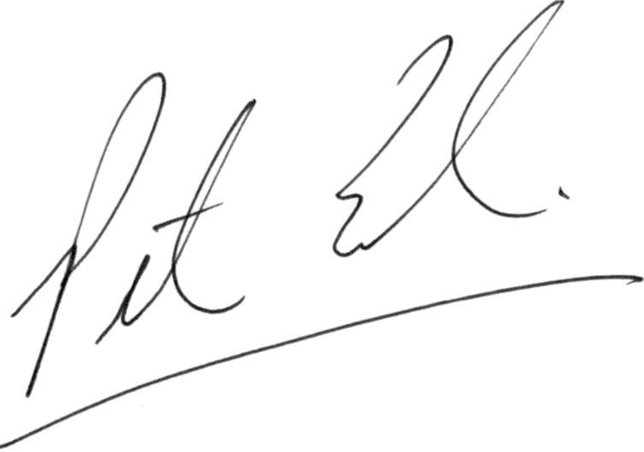

HOXTON MINI PRESS

INTRODUCTION: A TWIN'S PERSPECTIVE

Am I seeing double? Who's the eldest? Can you read each other's minds? Do you feel one another's pain?

These are just some of the questions us identical twins have learned to grin and bear. Perhaps you've even asked one of them yourself upon meeting a pair. You're not alone – since the dawn of time, humans have been fascinated by the mysterious phenomenon of twins. As a result, we find ourselves subjects of myth, superstition and literature.

The ancient city of Rome is named after Romulus, the twin brother of Remus and son of Mars, the god of war. Abandoned on a riverside, these twins were raised by a she-wolf. The image of the animal suckling the infants remains a symbol of the Italian capital today.

The Bible tells the story of Esau and Jacob, twin sons of Isaac and Rebekah. Esau, as the firstborn, stood to inherit the most but foolishly traded his birthright with his brother for a bowl of soup. Jacob, the smarter of the two, then disguised himself as his brother to trick his blind father into giving him his blessing. Perhaps this is the first recorded tale of twins playing tricks on their parents!

In some cultures twins are believed to possess supernatural powers. In rural areas of Madagascar, a mother of twins is expected to abandon the babies soon after birth to avoid a curse of bad luck from befalling the rest of the tribe. Others, such as the Bassa-Nge tribe in Nigeria regard twins as a divine blessing, harbingers of good luck and prosperity. This is just as well, as the country boasts the highest number of multiple births ever recorded, with the village of Igbo-Ora, north of Lagos earning itself the nickname 'The Twin Capital of the World'.

In modern fiction, representations of twinship are often exaggerated or even fetishised. Plots revolve around tales of mistaken identity, good versus evil, and shared love interests. Often we are portrayed as indistinguishable, one person in two bodies, with no real identity of our own. A common and unfair notion is that one is good and so, the other evil. Ask any set of twins which one is branded the 'evil twin' and no doubt they will give you a disgruntled answer.

The famous image of the Grady Twins in Stanley Kubrick's *The Shining*, holding hands and dressed doll-like in blue frills as they speak in unison is one that still unsettles the public psyche, and is perhaps responsible for cementing twins into the catalogue of foolproof horror-movie gimmicks. No doubt us twins stir the imagination and have the ability to unnerve and intrigue, but beyond our alluring exterior, what really lies at the heart of this unique relationship? Peter Zelewski's photographs certainly lend the outsider a rare and intimate insight.

It was by pure chance that ours and Peter's paths crossed.
We stumbled upon his work online, and like so many
others, were mesmerised by his striking street portraiture.
This project instantly struck a chord with us, not simply
because his subjects were identical twins, but because we
were drawn to his unembellished approach to capturing
our union.

Peter is a master of composition. His images portray with
only slight suggestion, the indelible bond between each
pair – we see a protective hand placed on a shoulder, a
possessive embrace, a shared mischievous grin – whilst
remaining refreshingly void of the cheesy mirror imagery
so common in twin photography. The symmetry lies in
his backgrounds; unintimate public settings such as a
park footpath, a concrete city walkway; stripped back
and bare, thus drawing the eye to the distinct differences
between the pairs. Some personalise their matching
outfits with jewellery, others opt for differentiating
hairstyles and tattoos, yet even without these subtle
markers their individuality shows through; it's in their
body language, their expressions.

Throughout the course of this project, Peter found that
his understanding of twinship developed beyond the
initial fascination that first evoked him:

'Meeting the twins became just as important and exciting
to me as the photography itself. I found myself moved and
inspired by their stories of the challenges and joys they'd
experienced. I felt as though I were being let into an elite
club, and luckily they were eager to invite me in. I'm only
just now able to comprehend how special and unique this
relationship is.'

It's true that few can understand the intrinsic bond
between twin siblings, who not only share an uncanny
resemblance, but also a profound and extraordinary
connection. Any parent or close friend of twins can testify
to this unbreakable union, a friendship which began in the
womb and continues to bind us together, like an invisible
thread linking one soul to the other. Ours is a guarded and
private world, but through Peter's lens you are invited to
take a glimpse inside.

Naomi and Alexandria Hewston, London 2018,
who appear on the last page of this book

PHOTOGRAPHER'S NOTE

'Why do you like photographing twins?' This was the question I was asked by almost every set I photographed. And the more I was asked this question the harder it was to provide a definitive answer. 'Because you all look so incredible!' was the obvious response, and although there was some truth in this, I think the real reason was rooted deeper than something purely visual.

It all started in my grade school days when my teacher introduced brothers Eric and Tim to the class. Up until this point, I had never met any identical twins but it was obvious there was something very special about these two. They had bags of confidence, tonnes of attitude but most importantly they had each other. I'm sure there was a certain amount of jealousy on my part upon witnessing this strong, special bond which seemed to invisibly unite the twins – a bond I longed for but rarely shared with my own older brother.

Years later and now turning my attention to photography, my twins fascination surfaced again with the discovery of photographer Diane Arbus and her portrait of twins Cathleen and Colleen Wade. The image was strong, powerful, intriguing and somewhat disturbing – it fascinated me. I then discovered the work of August Sander, Mary Ellen Mark and Roger Ballen, who also took iconic portraits of twins at some point in their careers. As my fascination grew I knew the next portrait I took was going to be of twins.

My mission was simple: to meet and photograph as many identical twins as possible. I initially approached them as strangers on the street, then I contacted people through social media. As a result, I have photographed twins of many different nationalities, young and old. I was thrilled with the portraits I was taking and equally excited about the stories the twins shared with me. I was moved to tears by Hermon and Heroda when they told me they both lost their hearing aged just seven, and I came out in fits of laughter upon hearing how Yasmin attempted to take a photo of her sister Laila on her phone, but because of their incredible likeness, ended up taking a selfie.

The one thing the twins all shared was that they all felt privileged and proud to be part of this elite club, a club they wholeheartedly welcomed me into.

After four years, the time came when I needed to close the chapter on this project. I can now proudly look through the pages of this book at some of the strongest, most visually compelling and enjoyable portraits I have taken. I will remember every set of twins I photographed and the stories they shared with me. I would like to take this opportunity to thank and dedicate this book to all the twins – without your co-operation, dedication, enthusiasm and of course your ability to 'look so incredible' this book wouldn't have been possible.

Peter Zelewski, London 2018

PETER ZELEWSKI

Peter Zelewski is a London-based portrait and documentary photographer. Born in Detroit, USA, he moved to London in the 1980s and studied at the London College of Communication (LCC). His portraiture concentrates primarily on the exploration of people, culture and urban life. Zelewski's work has been featured in numerous publications, he has won several awards and been a prizewinner in the Taylor Wessing Photographic Portrait Prize. His previous book, *People of London*, was also published by Hoxton Mini Press. Zelewski is not, nor ever has been, an identical twin.

HOXTON MINI PRESS

Hoxton Mini Press is a small but award-winning independent publisher based in East London. They make collectable photography books focusing on niche subjects and human stories. As more of the world goes online they believe that books should be cherished as beautiful physical objects that earn their place on well-managed shelves and are passed down through generations. Hoxton Mini Press was started by Ann and Martin, and their two dogs, Moose and Bug. Moose and Bug are brothers but not twins.

KIRA & TAYA

15 years old, Taya older by 2 minutes

'Growing up we were so close that we never felt the need to have lots of friends but now we would love to have a best friend other than each other. The problem is that when we meet someone new they always see us as one and not as individuals. Our individual identity is really important to us.'

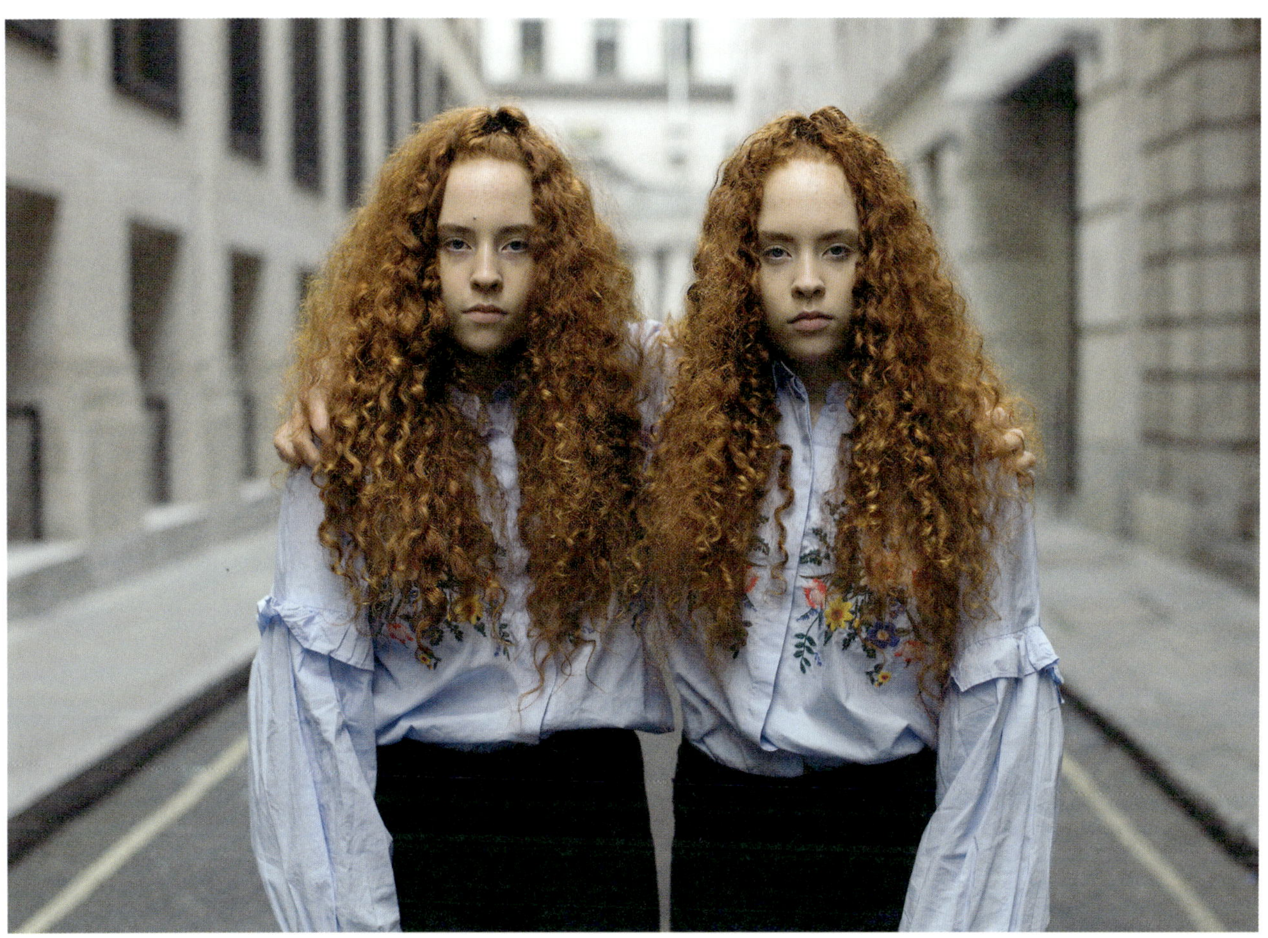

ALAN & GARY

37 years old, Alan older by 20 minutes

'We argue over the stupidest things. Last week Gary ordered the wrong pizza: it was supposed to have tomato sauce on it and he ordered garlic sauce. Who orders garlic sauce on pizza?! I went mad and we didn't speak for two days.'

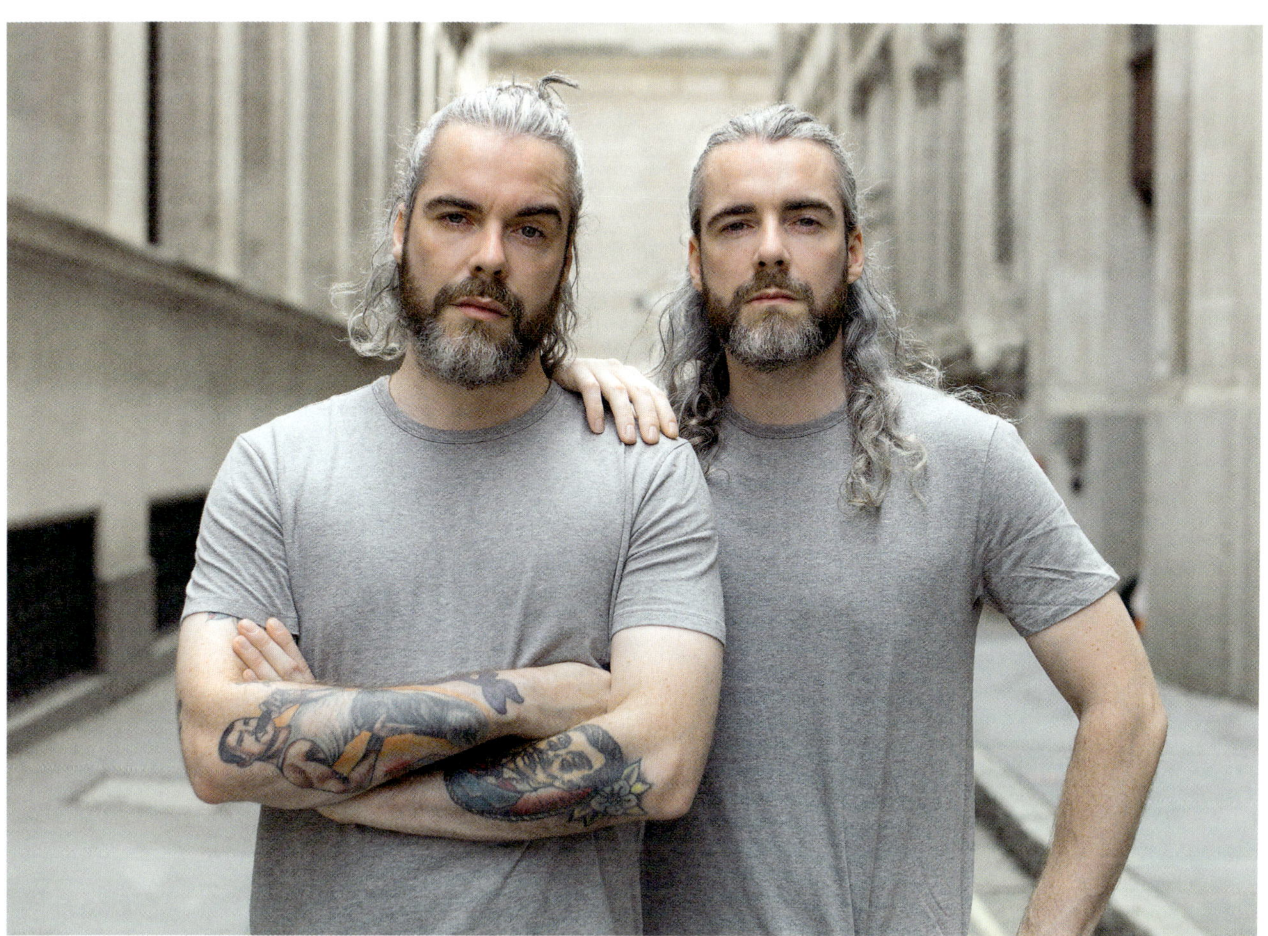

LILIBET & LITIANA

8 years old, Lilibet older by 3 minutes

'Our mum told us that when we were born we were placed in a small cot in the hospital lying next to each other. While Lilibet was having her nappy changed I woke to realise that, for the first time, she wasn't next to me. I started crying and our mum quickly placed Lilibet back down next to me and I immediately stopped. I started stroking Lilibet's face and we later found out that she had a large hole in her heart that required surgery. It was as if I knew that my twin needed protecting.'

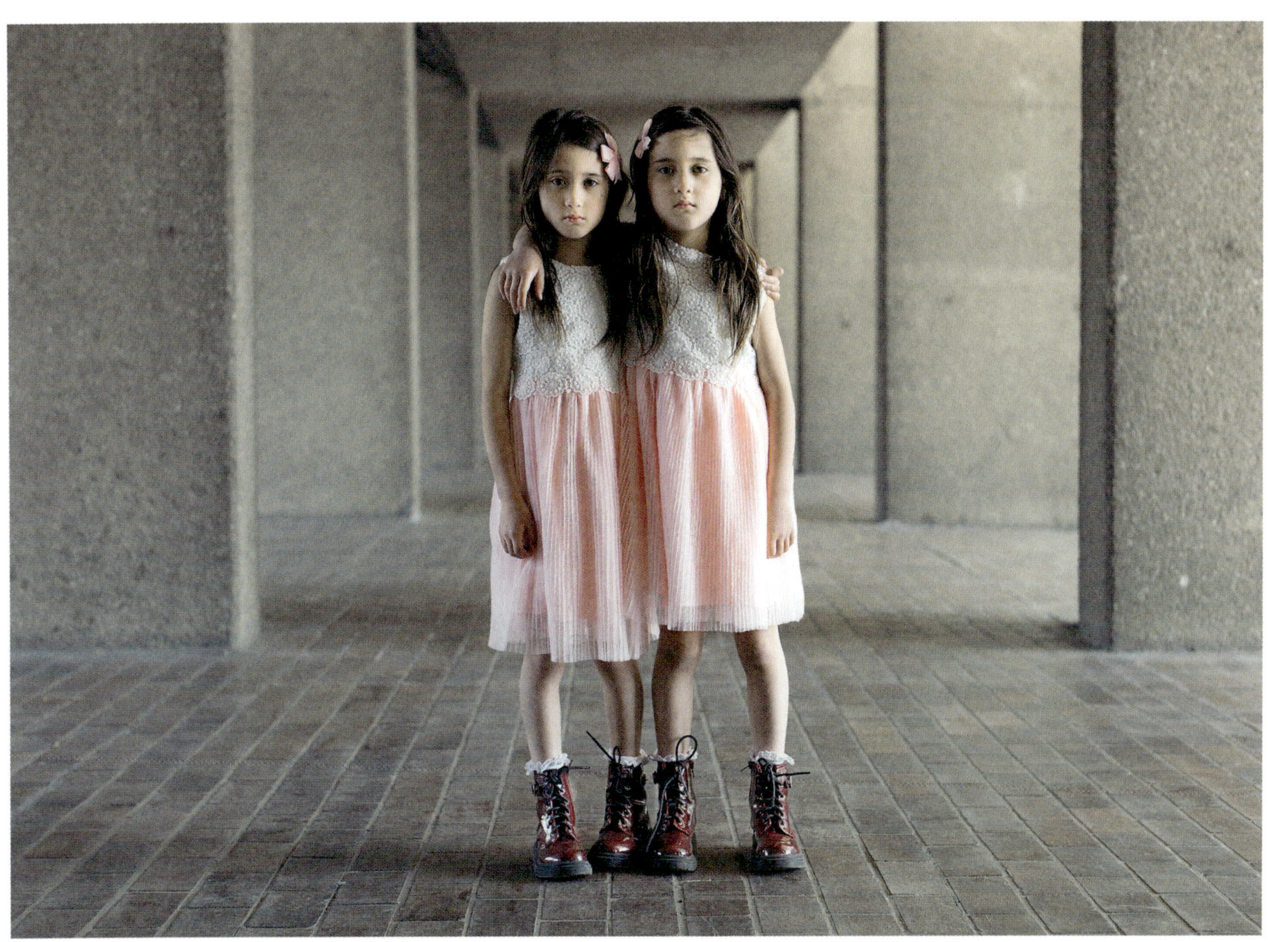

EMILY & SOPHIE

15 years old, Sophie older by 2 minutes

'Sophie is always stealing my clothes. She drives me crazy because she always denies it. Unfortunately, although I have grown two inches taller in the last few months, we're still the same size so I can't see things changing any time soon.'

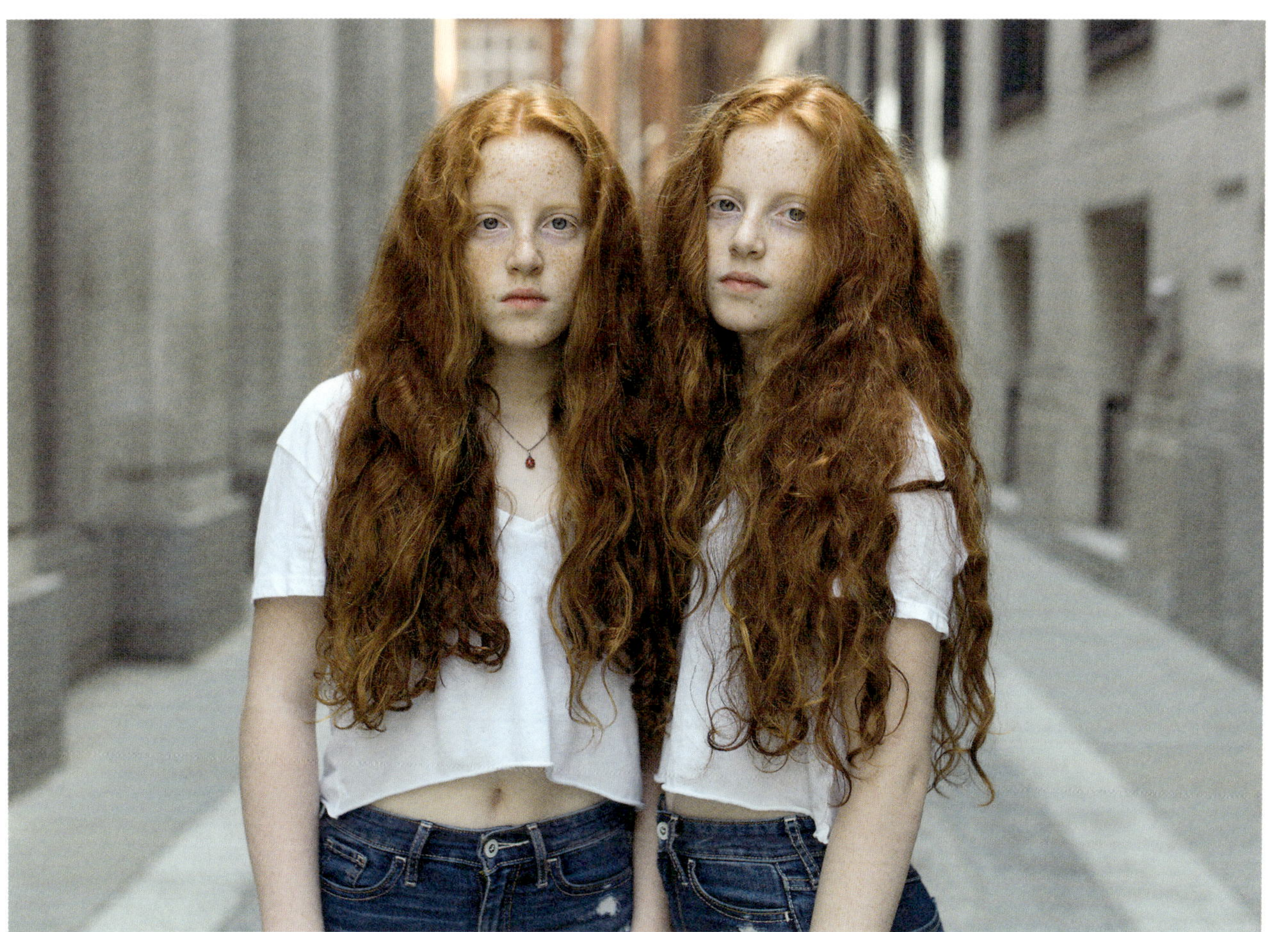

HERMON & HERODA

35 years old, Hermon older by 1 minute

'We were born in Eritrea, Africa, and moved to London when we were seven years old to seek medical help after we both became deaf at the same time. Our disability has brought us closer together; we have an unbreakable, special bond that unites the two of us. We finish each other's sentences, read each other's minds and feel each other's pain. Yes, it's real.'

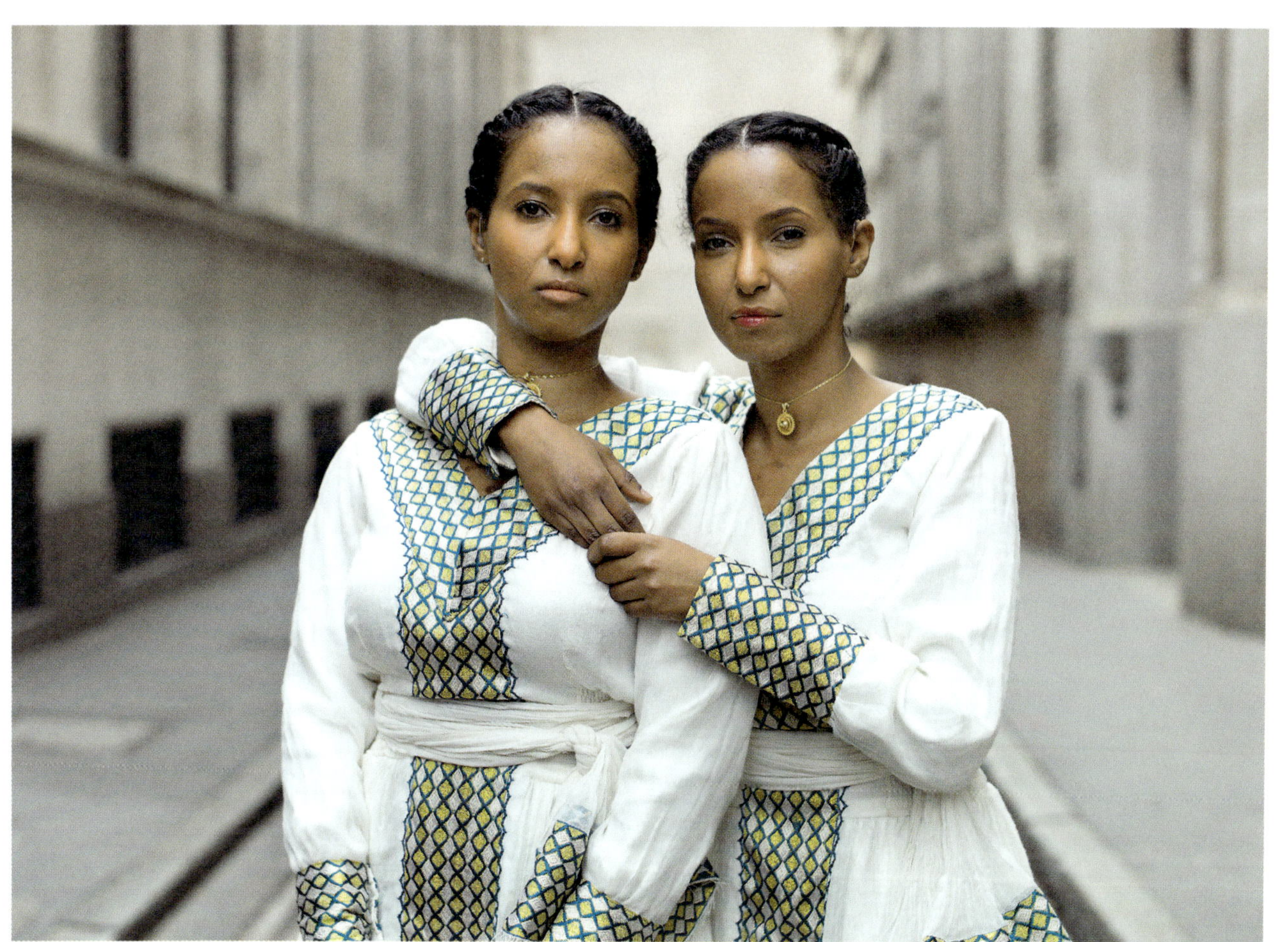

SHARMEENA & RIDHWANA

23 years old, Sharmeena older by 2 minutes

'Both Sharmeena and I have moved around so much in our lives – we have never really lived in a place we could call home. Making friends has been hard but we've always had each other.'

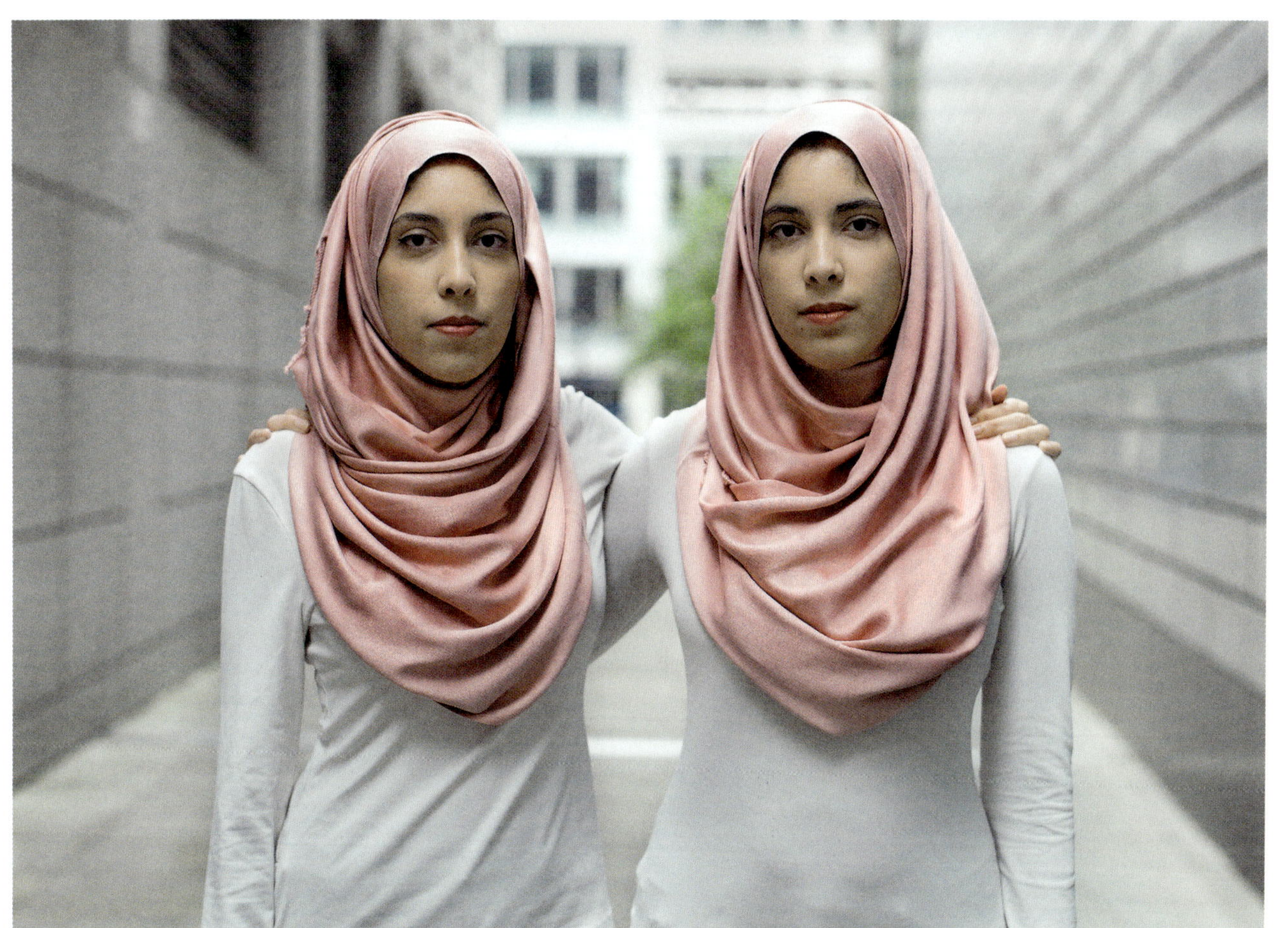

MICKEY & REGGIE

2 years old, Mickey older by 2 minutes

'As Mickey and Reggie's parents, we are glad our sons are twins because we know they'll both have a best friend for life. As they grow older, we hope their bond will provide the security and confidence to ensure that whatever goals they pursue, the other will always be there to say, "I'm proud of you".'

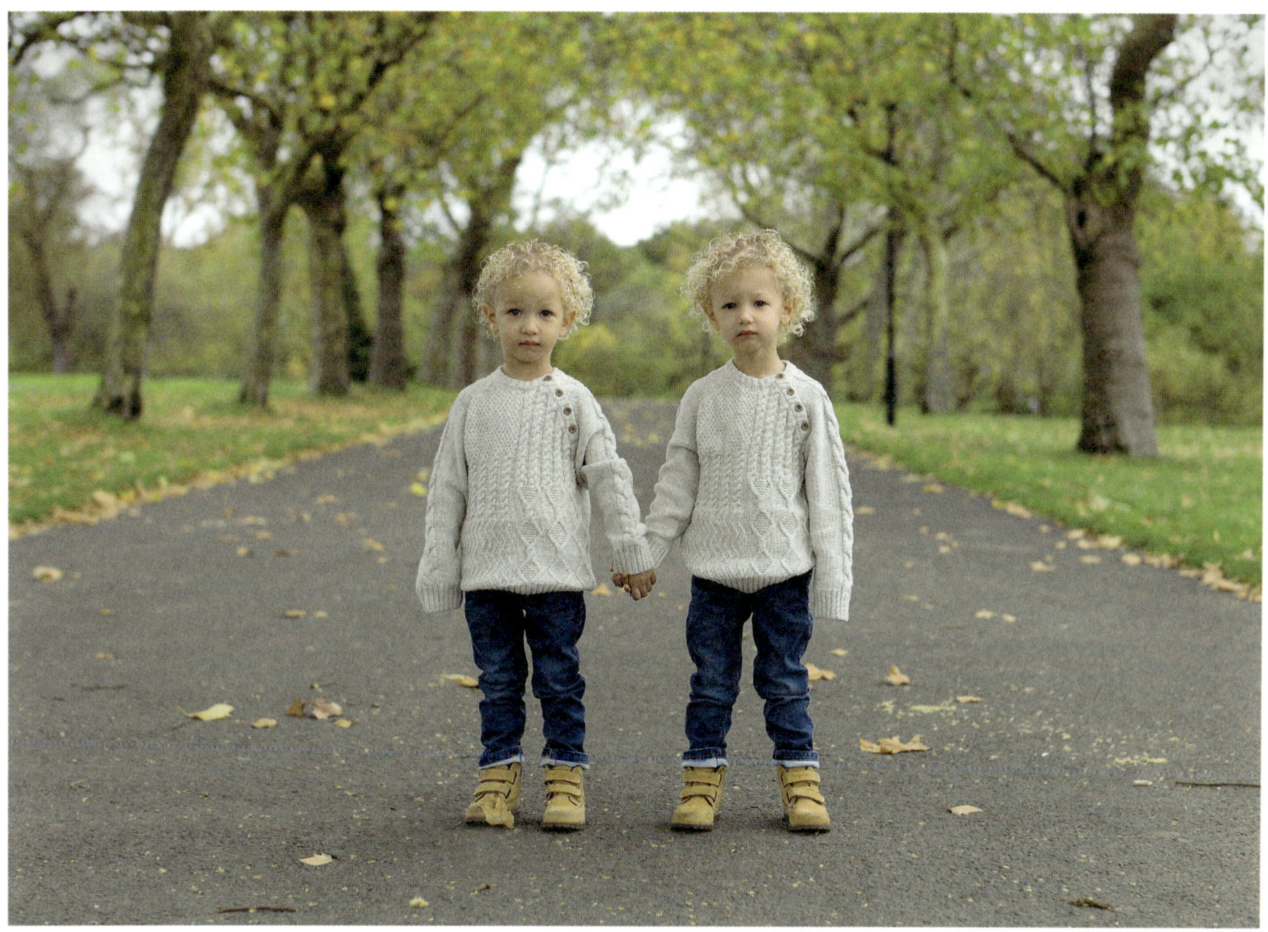

DELILAH & TULLULAH

13 years old, Delilah older by 2 minutes

'People always ask the same question – "What's it like to be a twin?" – but how can we answer that when we don't know what it's like *not* to be a twin?'

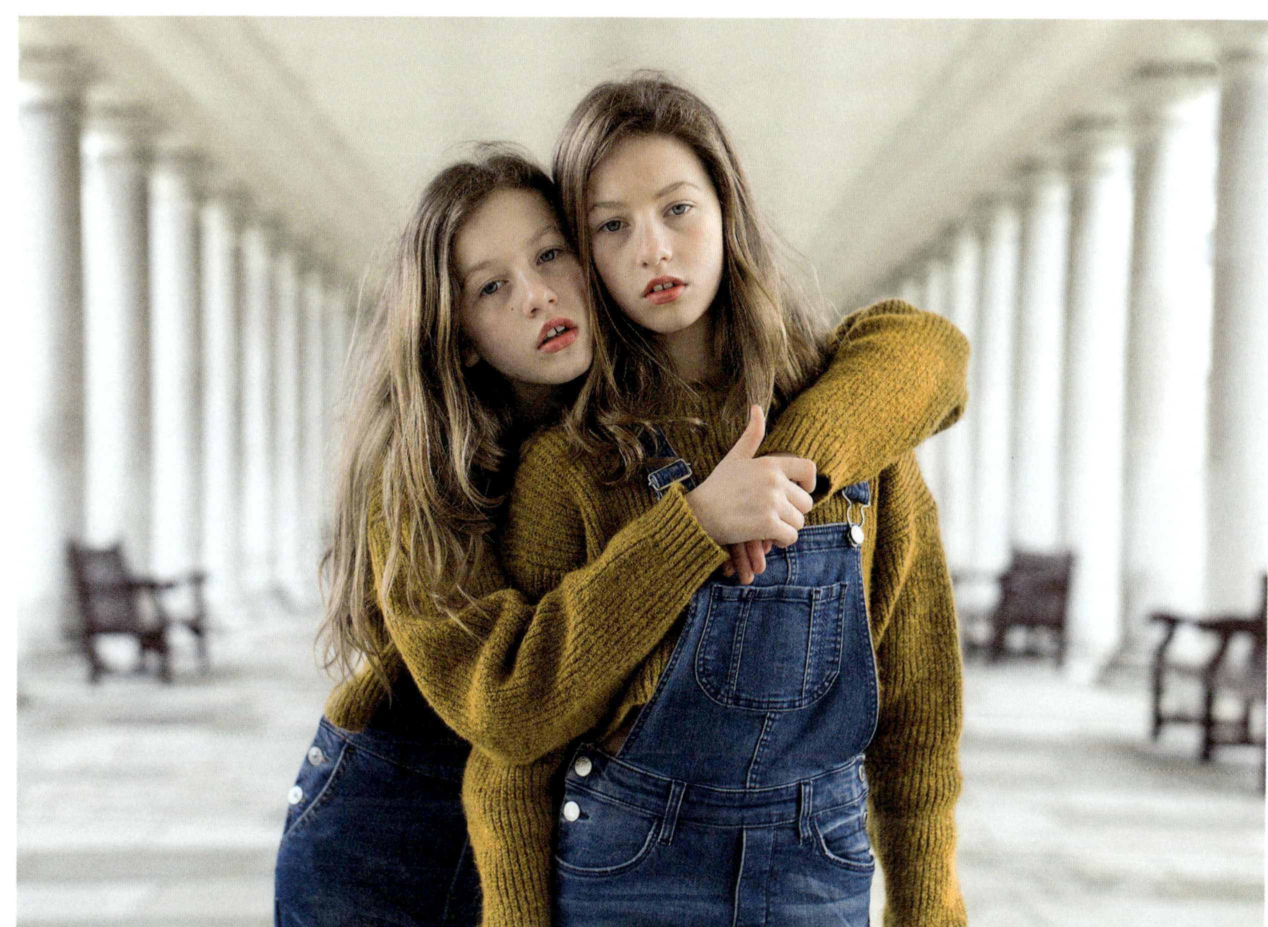

LEE & CLINTON

23 years old, Clinton older by 7 minutes

'We dressed the same from a very early age. This never went down well with our teachers at school; they hated our unity and tried their best to keep us apart. We still dress alike today. Whenever we go shopping we always pick up two of everything.'

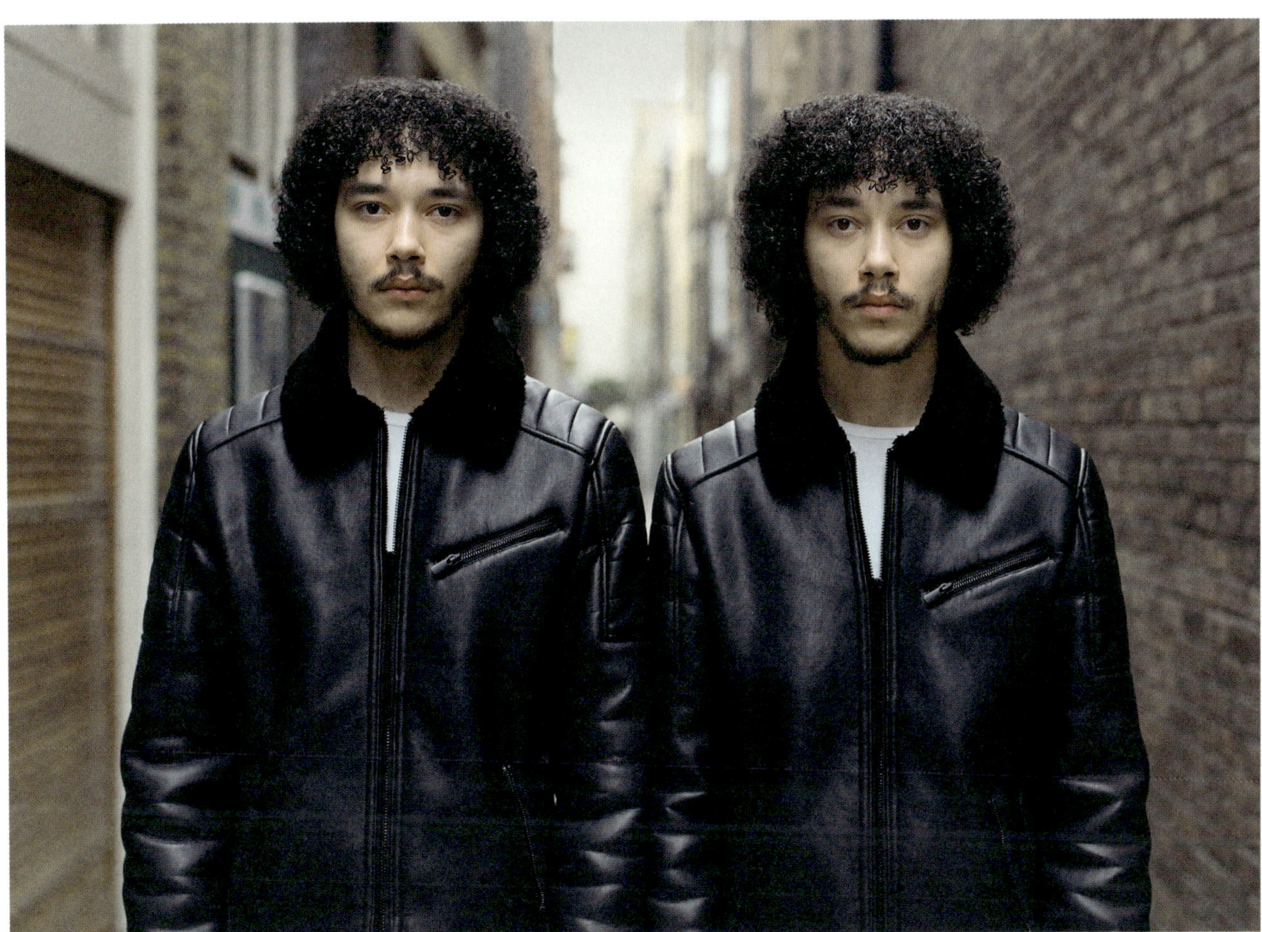

WENDY & GAYE

56 years old, Wendy older by 4 minutes

'I am the doer in our relationship, the dominant one, whereas Gaye just follows me. She makes me so angry sometimes but she's my best friend at the end of the day, the only one who can put me in my place.'

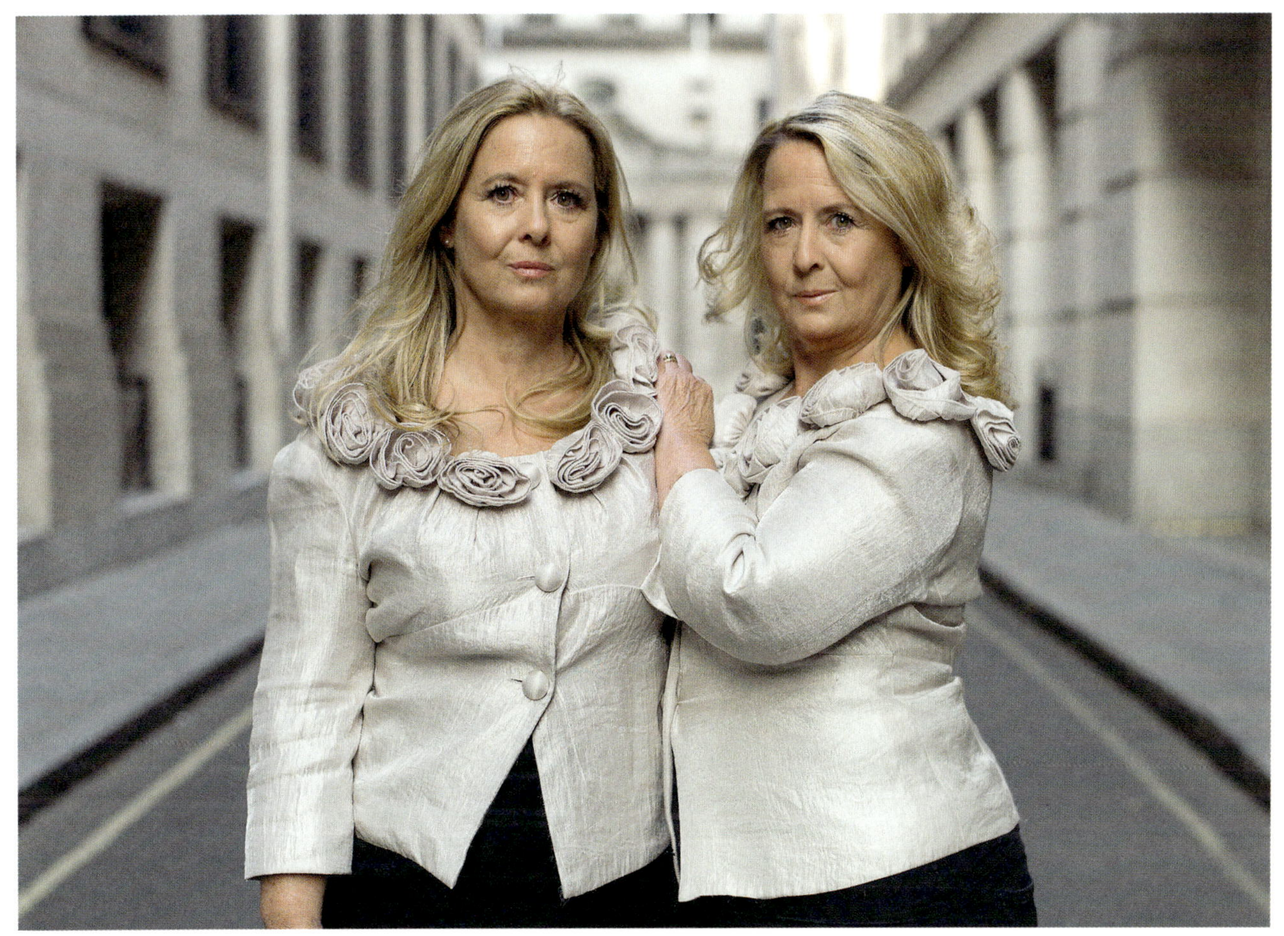

OLLIE & MATTIE

12 years old, Mattie older by 59.1 seconds

'As babies our mum used to put us to sleep in the same cot but made sure that there was lots of room between us. Every morning she would wake up to see that we had moved so close together that our heads were touching. Even now, we still prefer to sleep in the same bed. We feel closer, more secure that way.'

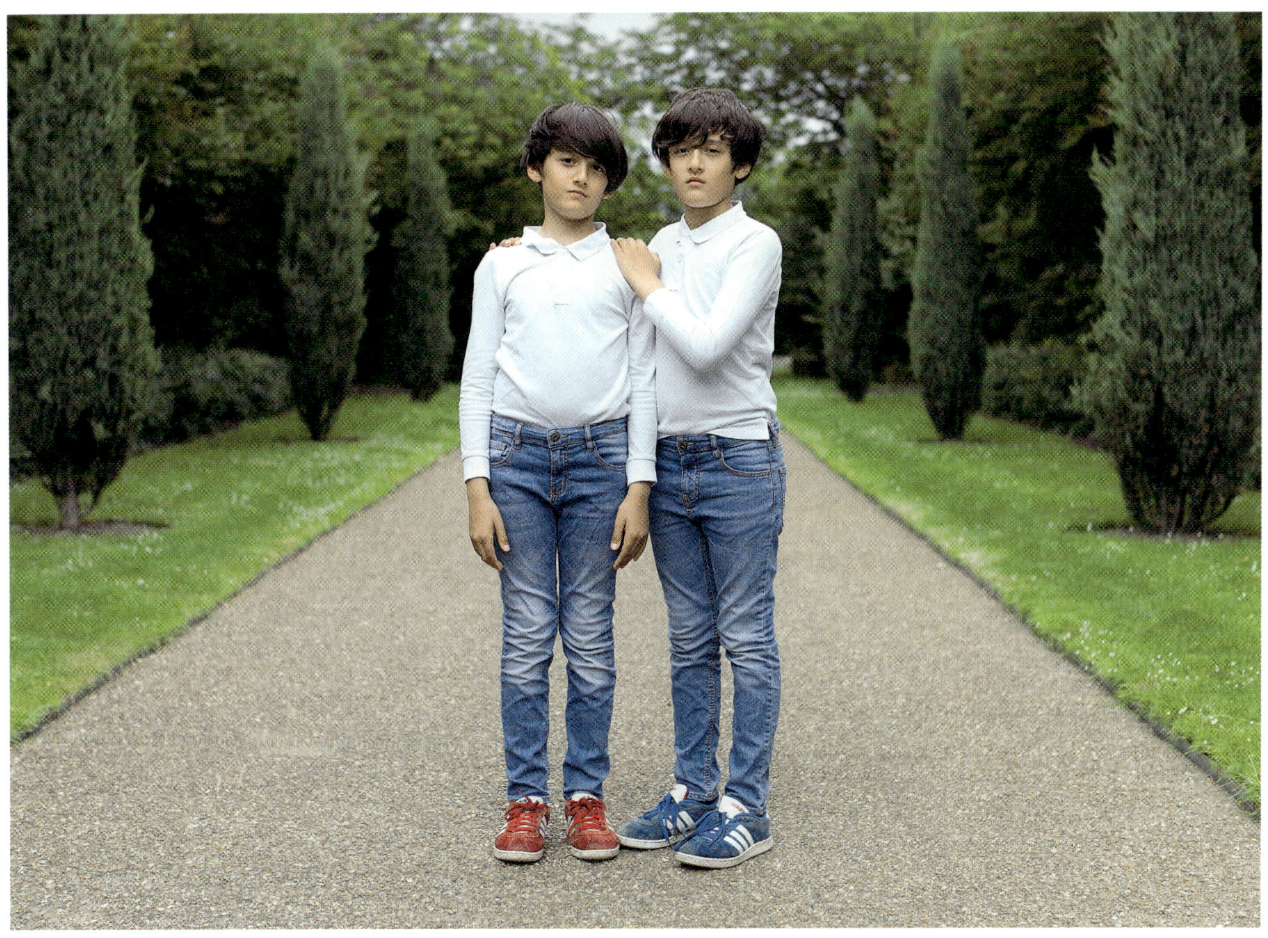

CHÉ & LEONIE

23 years old, Ché older by 2 minutes

'It has been tough for both of us. Our mother was an addict and our dad died from an overdose just weeks before we were born. He was only 16. We were placed in care from an early age and we had no one else but each other.'

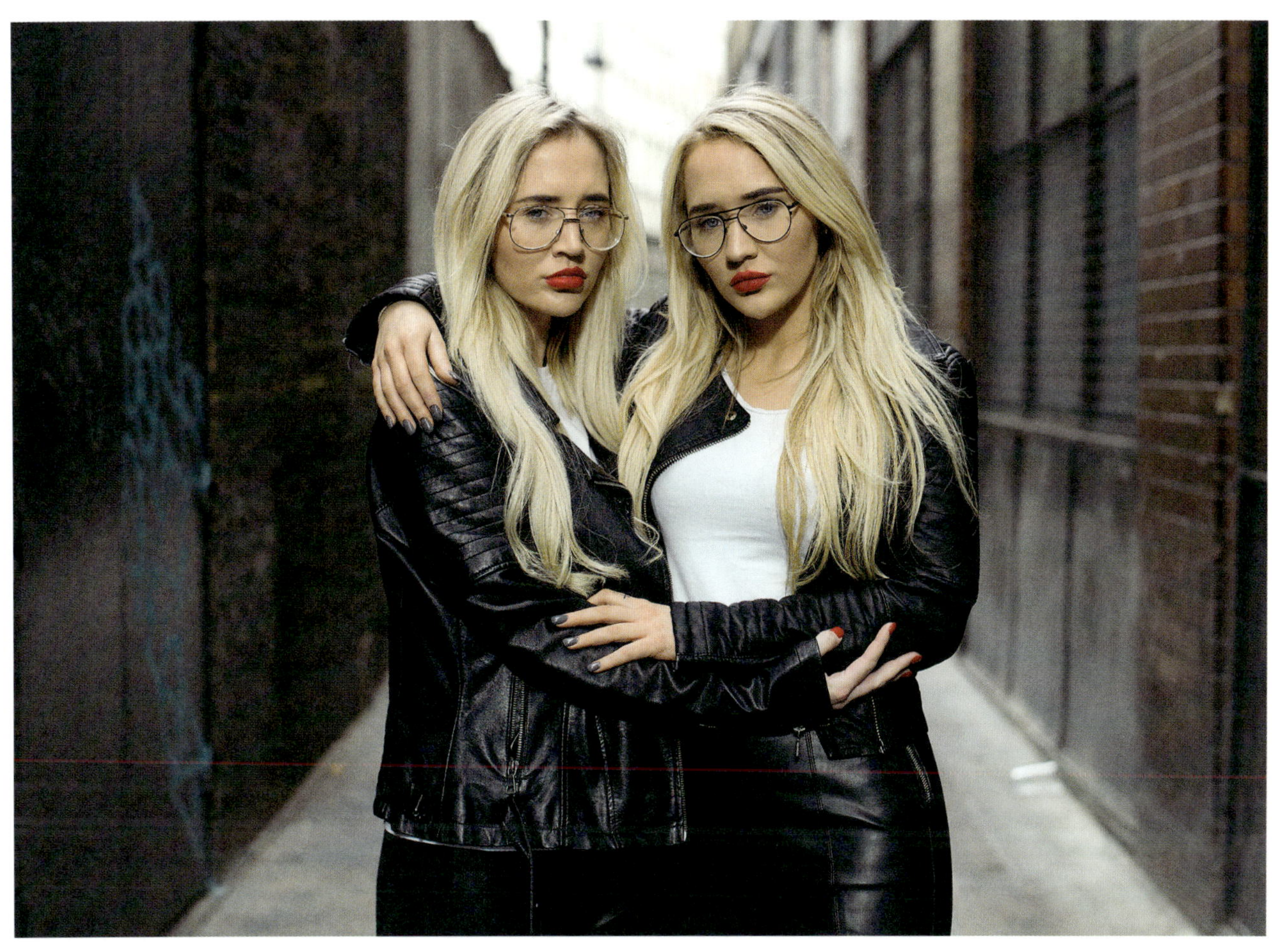

LEAH & CHLOE

13 years old, Leah older by 1 minute

'Chloe once fell from the top of our bunk bed and broke her collarbone. Even though she was in terrible pain she didn't cry once but I couldn't stop crying. It was as if her pain had transferred to me. I knew exactly how she was feeling.'

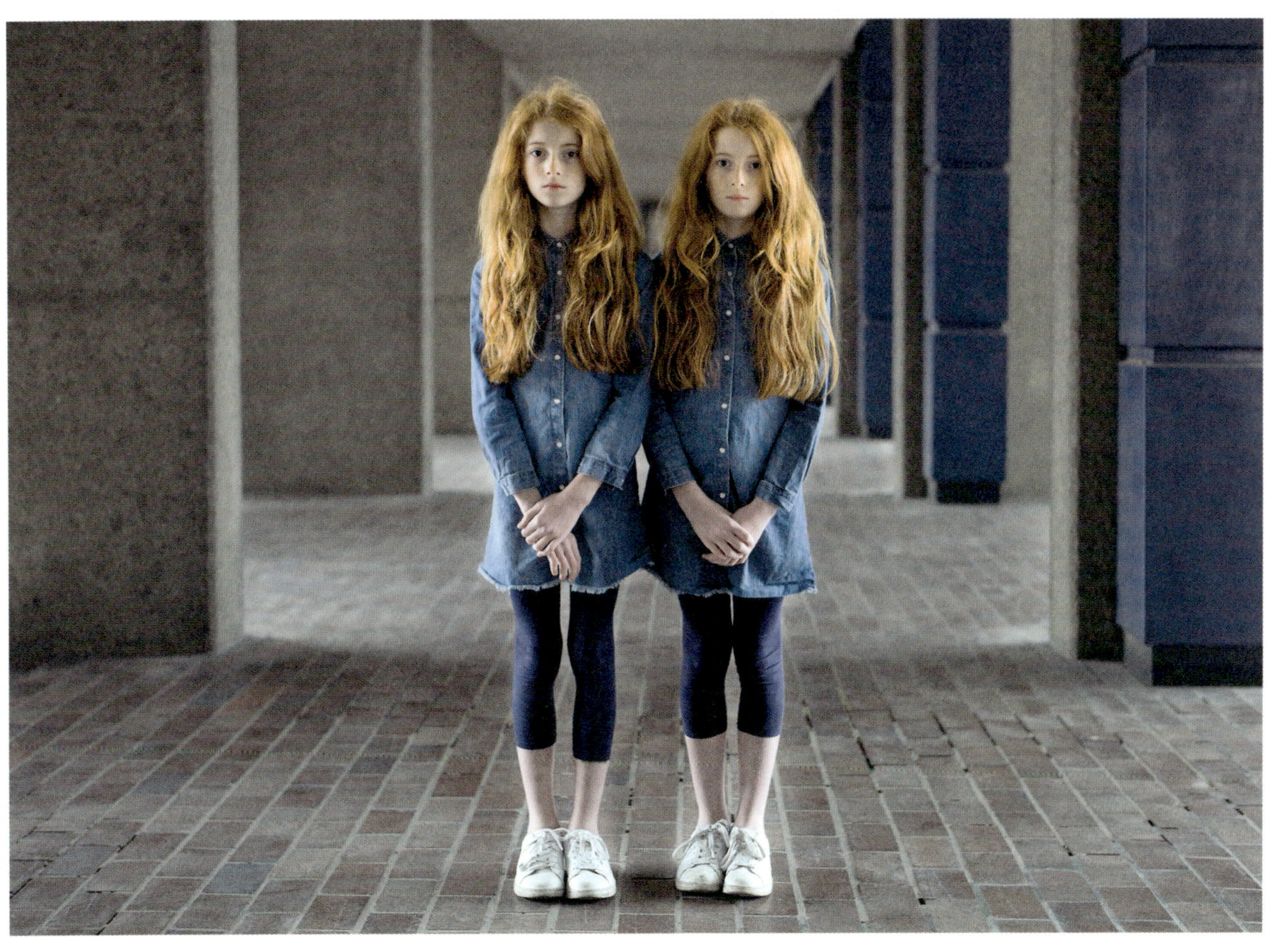

DEVONTAY & DIJON

23 years old, Devontay older by 1 minute

'We love being twins. The only downside is that when we are apart friends often mistakenly approach the "other" twin which gets really embarrassing when you have no idea who they are.'

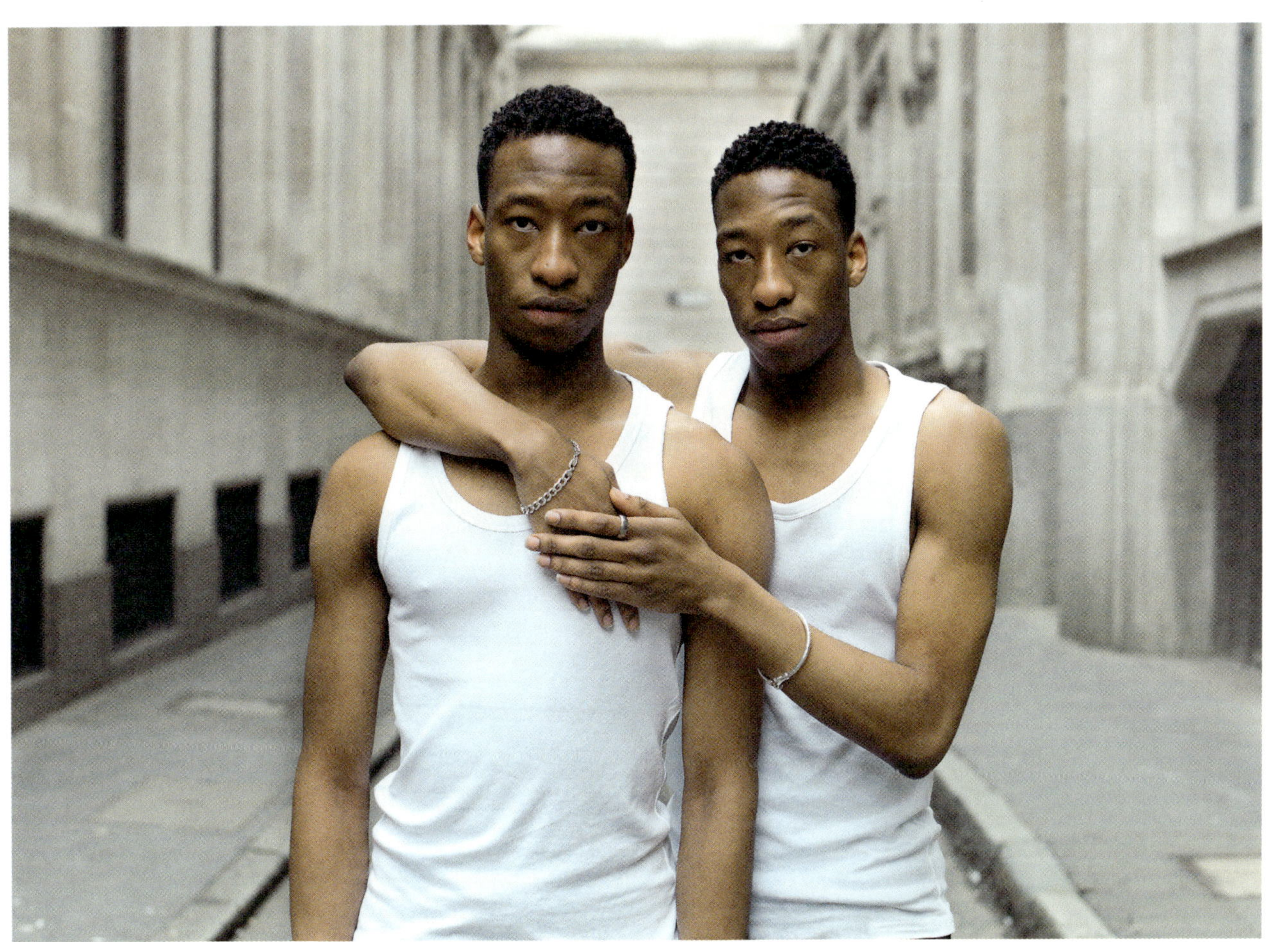

POLLY & SOPHIE

31 years old, Sophie older by 30 seconds

'We can unlock each other's iPhones because we have almost identical fingerprints. We are a rare breed of identical twins called "monozygotic twins" and have virtually indistinguishable DNA. We would be a forensic expert's biggest nightmare.'

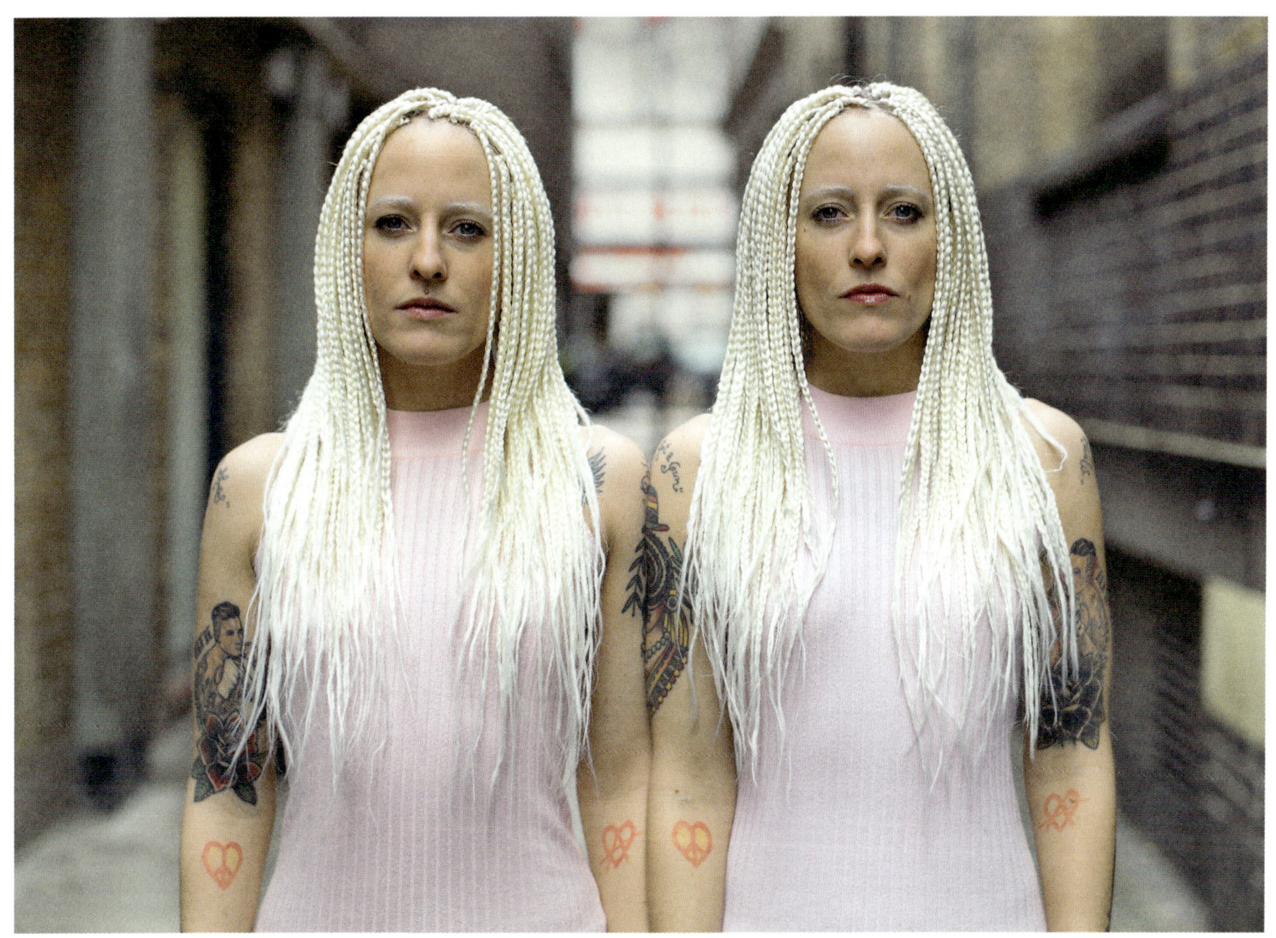

ORLA & CLARA

7 years old, Orla older by 1 minute

'Together we are fearless, whenever one of us is scared we will always be there for the other. The best thing about being a twin is that we always have someone to play with.'

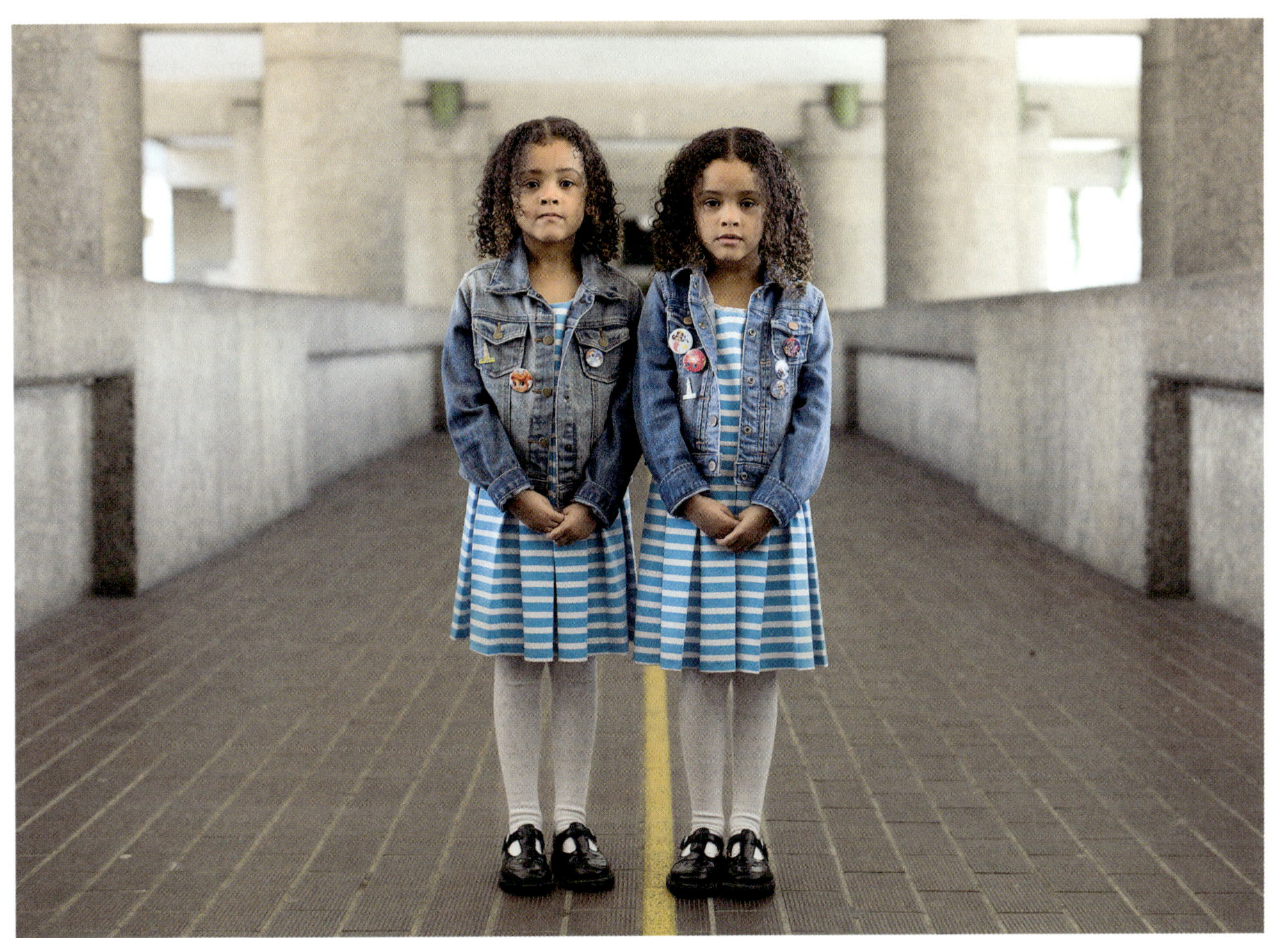

JOAO & EDMUNDO

23 years old, Joao older by 10 minutes

'Our parents were born in Portugal but we were born in the South of France and have spent most of our lives there. England is our home now. This is where we want to stay.'

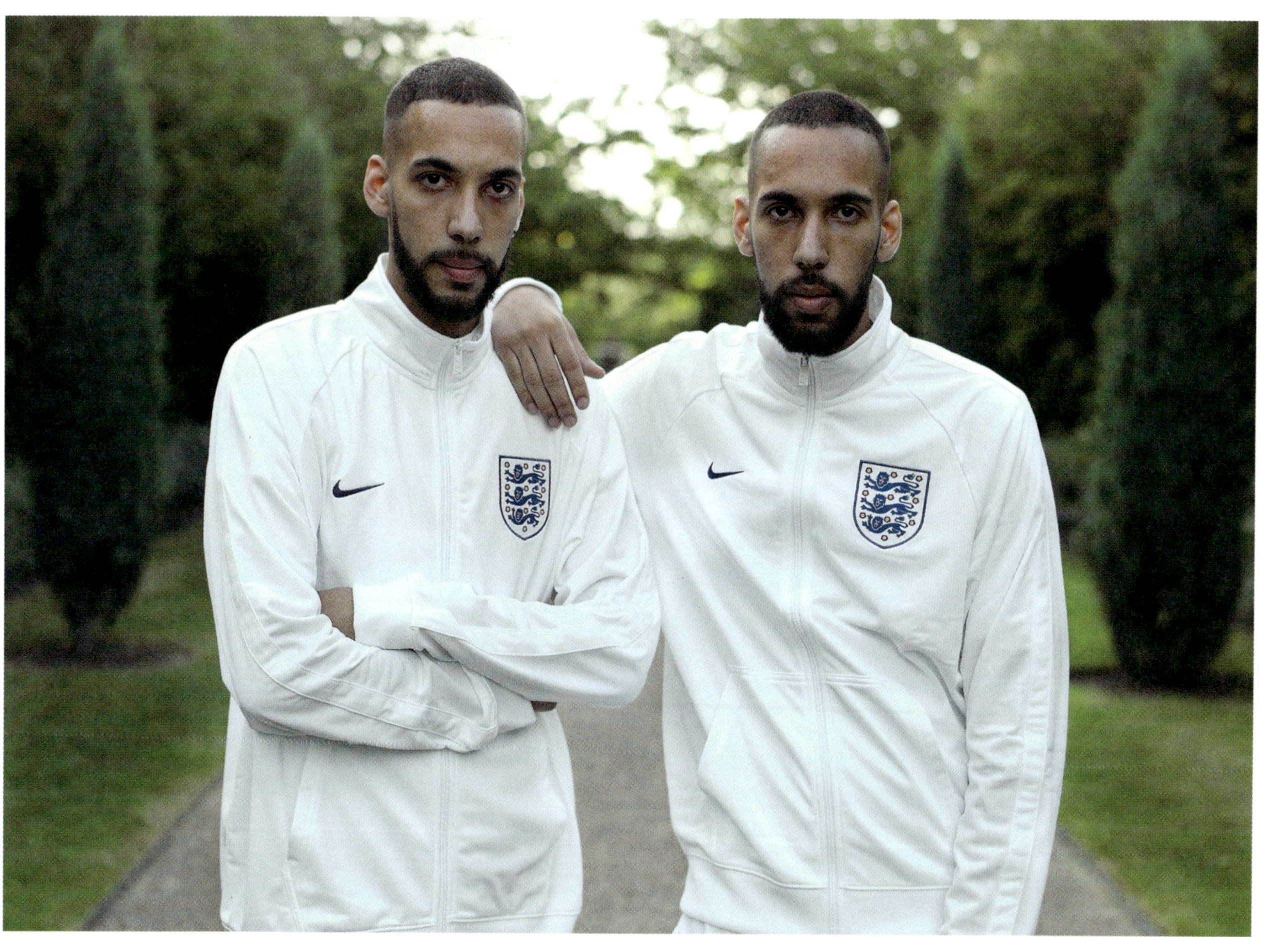

JOE & DUKE

15 years old, Duke older by 1 minute

'Joe is flamboyant and wants to be a makeup artist one day whereas I love photography and prefer to stay behind the scenes. The best thing about being a twin is being able to talk comfortably with each other and never having to worry about being judged.'

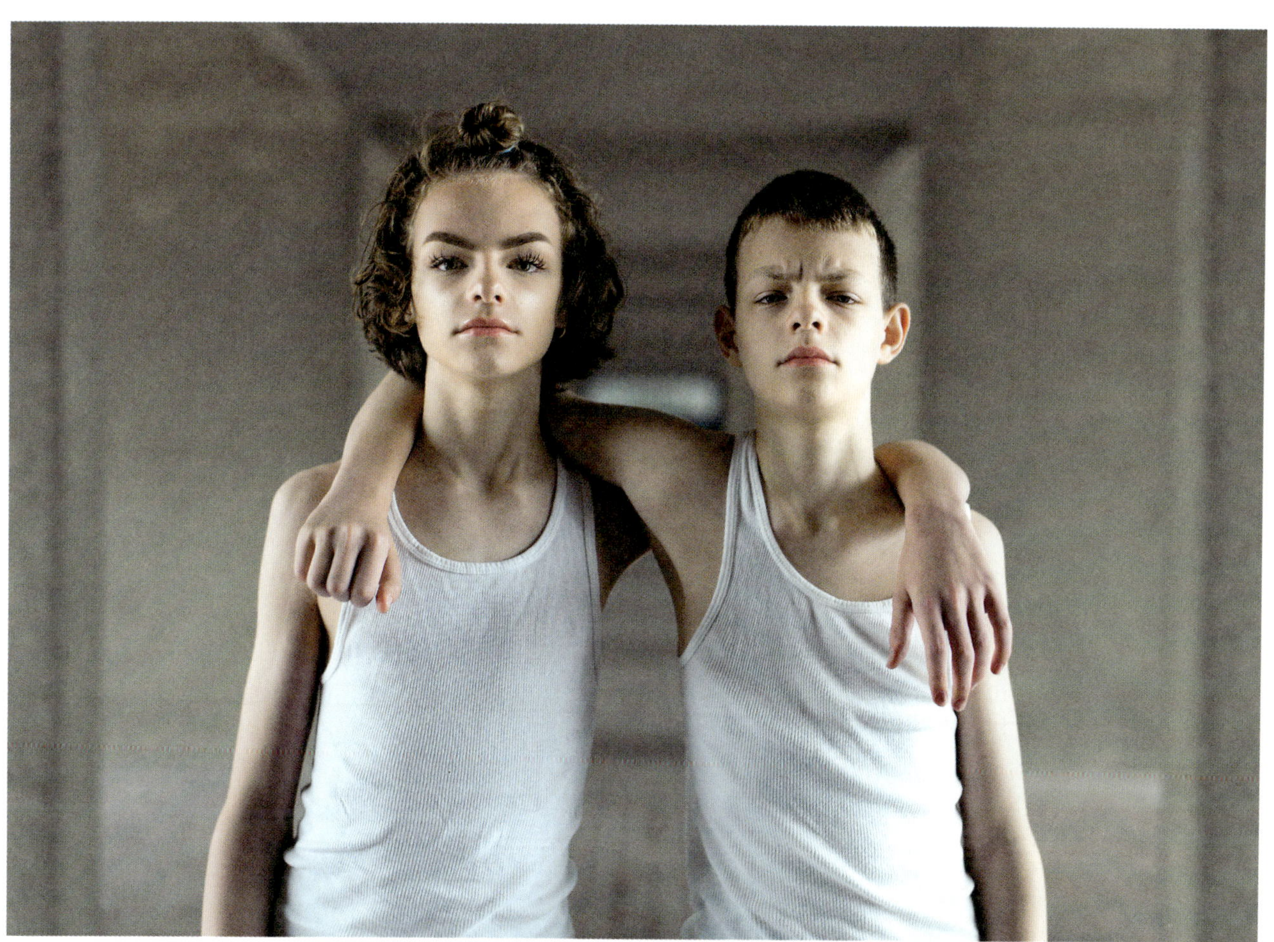

CHRISTINA & GEORGINA

30 years old, Georgina older by 9 minutes

'When we were younger we constantly argued about petty things, especially when it came to tidying our shared bedroom. We would spend hours trying to decide who should clean what percentage of the room.'

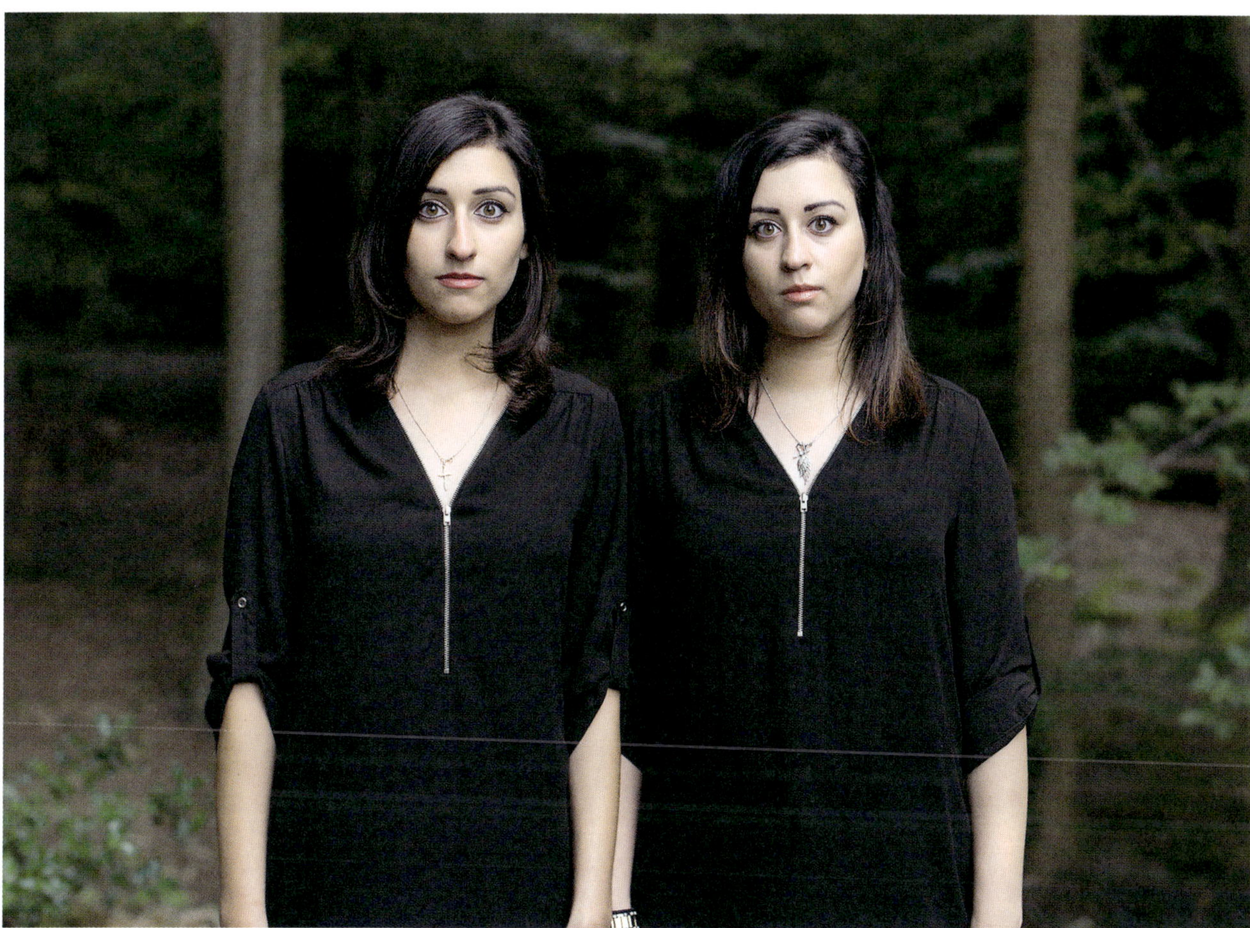

CALLUM & MAX

7 years old, Callum older by 2 minutes

'Our mum calls us her "Miracle Boys" because we were born 12 weeks early and weighed only 2lbs 5oz. The doctor said we were so tiny it would take a miracle to keep us alive. We must have good genes because our grandad was a twin and so was his mum.'

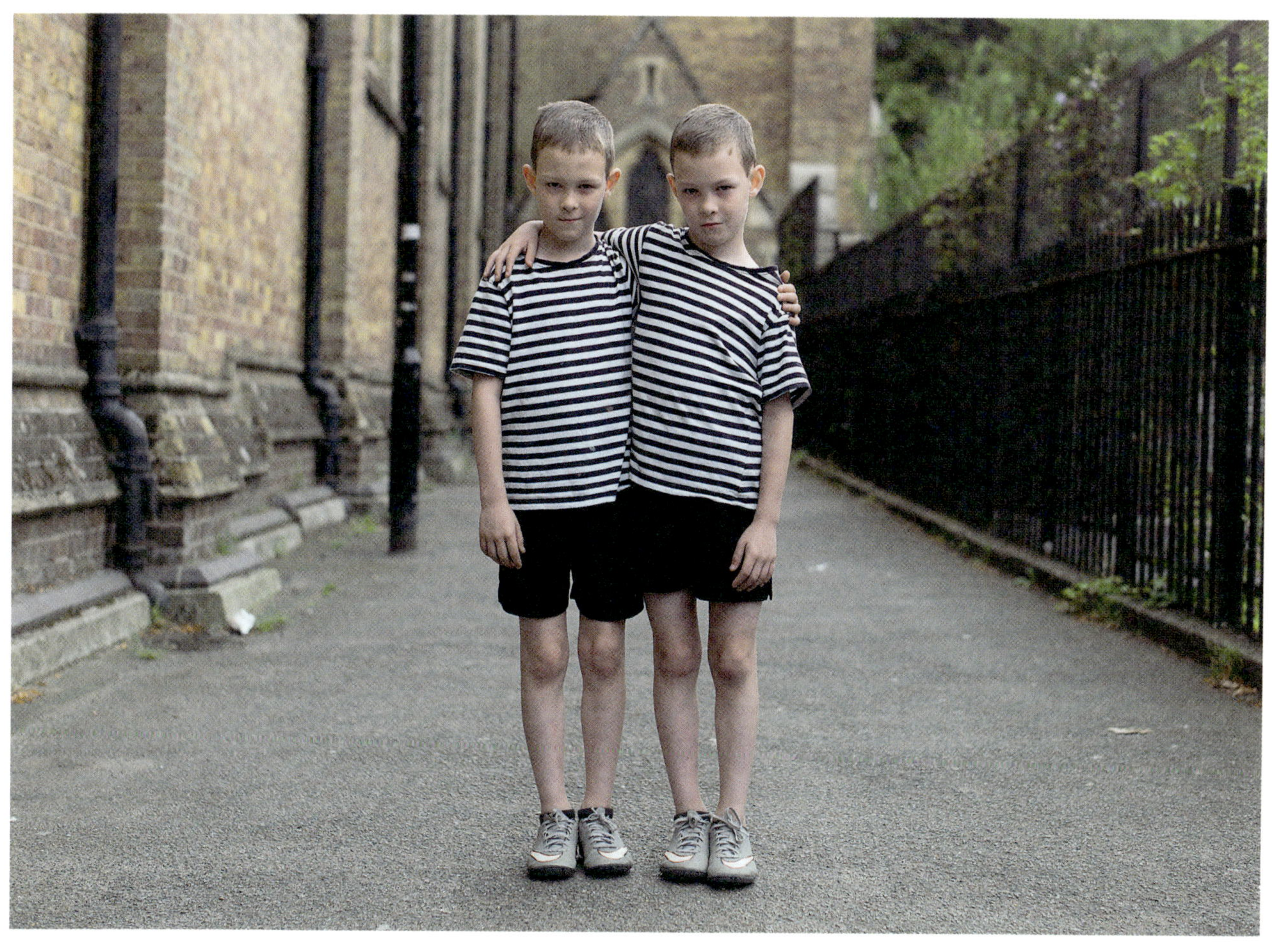

CRISTIAN & GEORGE

33 years old, George older by 5 minutes

'Getting married was really difficult because I realised it was going to be the first time George and I would be properly separated. When I proposed to my wife I had to sit down with her and explain that my brother would always take priority. She found it hard to accept at first but understands now.'

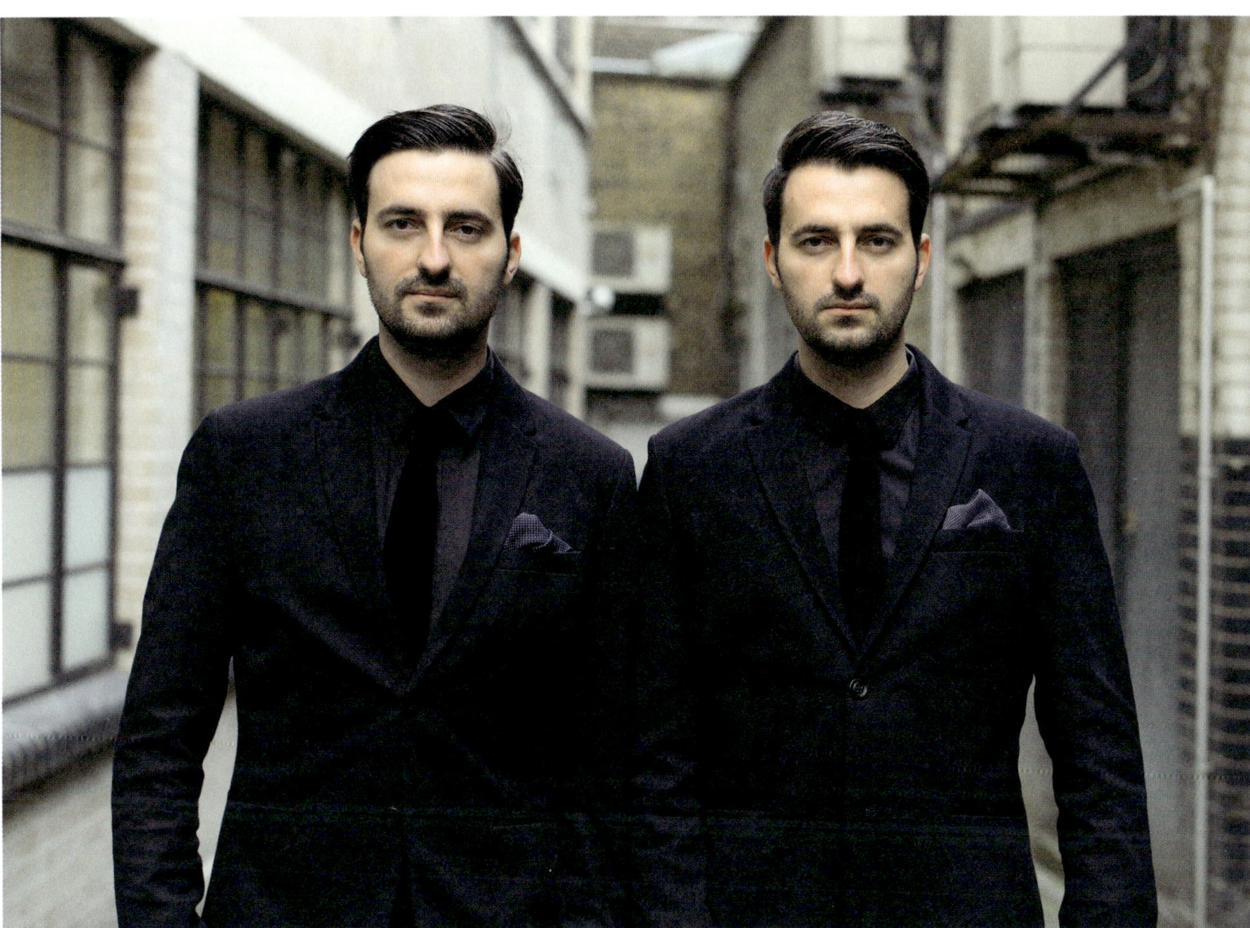

JADZIA & TESSIE

57 years old, Jadzia older by 30 minutes

'We worked at Woolworths together in the late 1970s and used to have endless hours of fun playing tricks on people. The store manager was so fed up with the attention we would get from customers that he eventually separated us so that we couldn't work next to each other.'

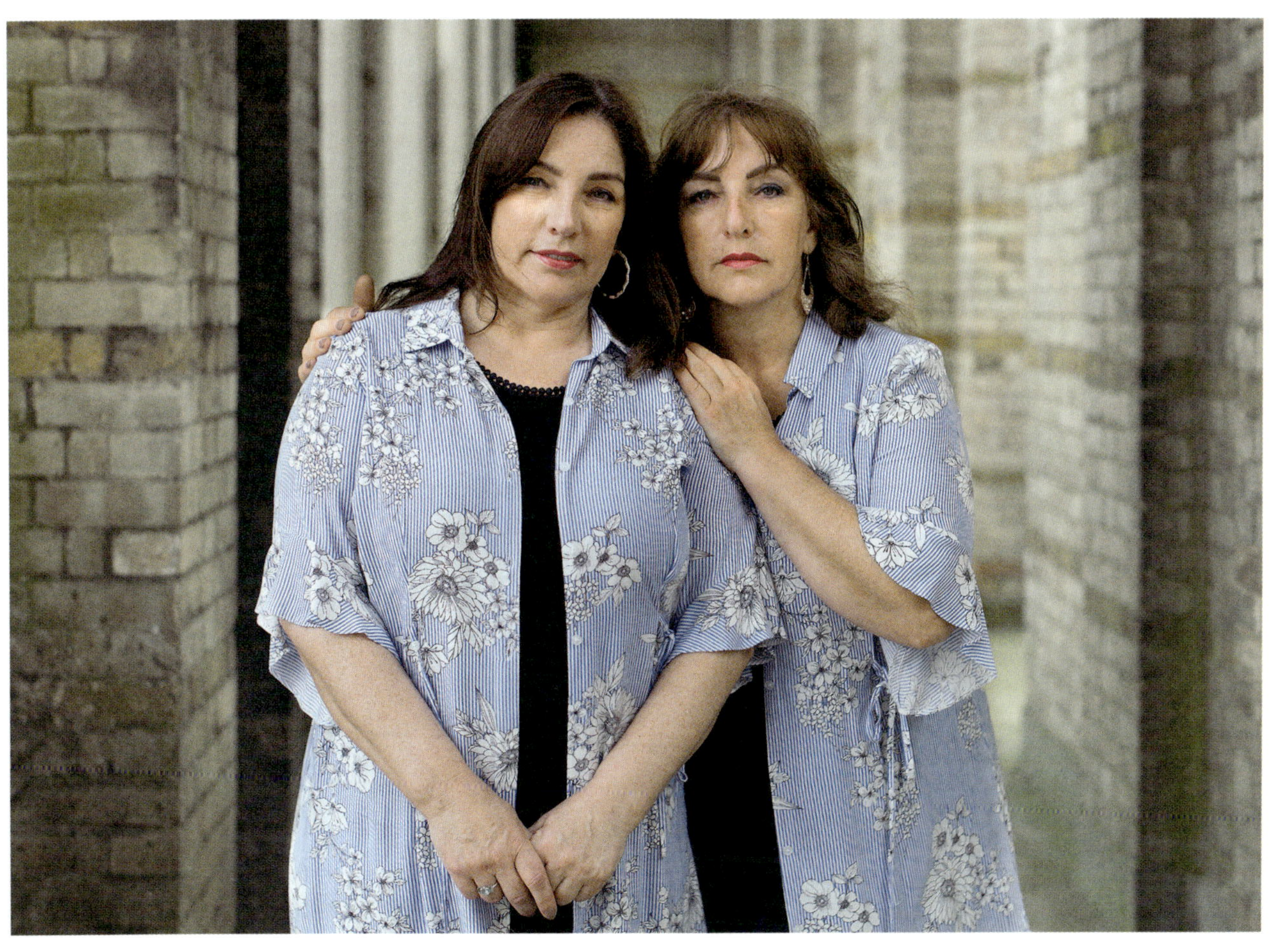

JOANNA & SUSANDJO

23 years old, Joanna older by 1 minute

'Last week we argued over something really petty and refused to sit together on the train. Joanna is the stubborn one – she moved five rows back. The argument only lasted 20 minutes and soon she was back in the seat next to me.'

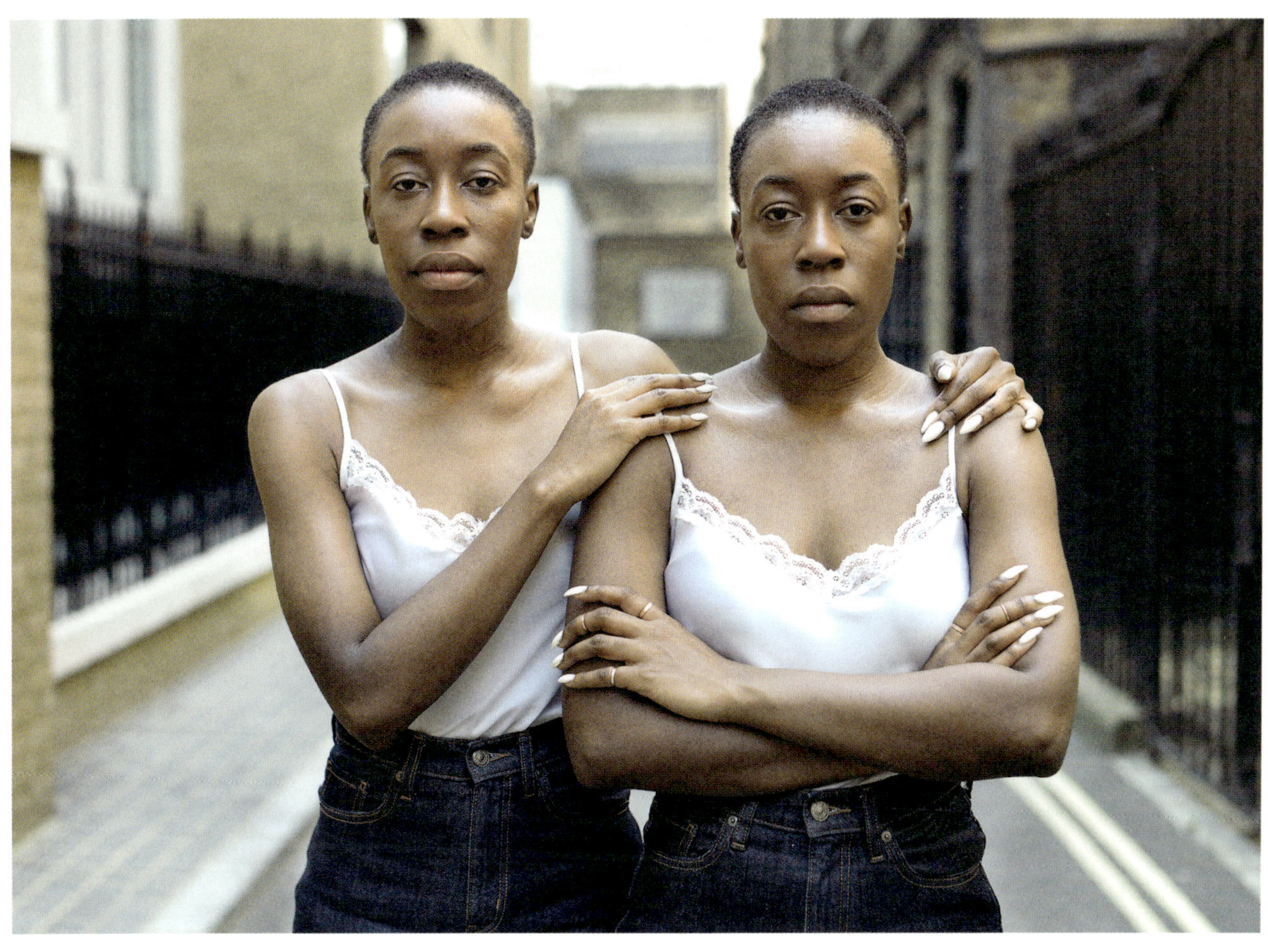

DAWN & HEATHER

18 years old, Dawn older by 26 minutes

'I remember in our primary school play we were cast as two crazy twins called Axel and Throttle who lived in a cottage made out of candy. I find it interesting how the most comedic characters were twins. It was inevitable that we were chosen to play them.'

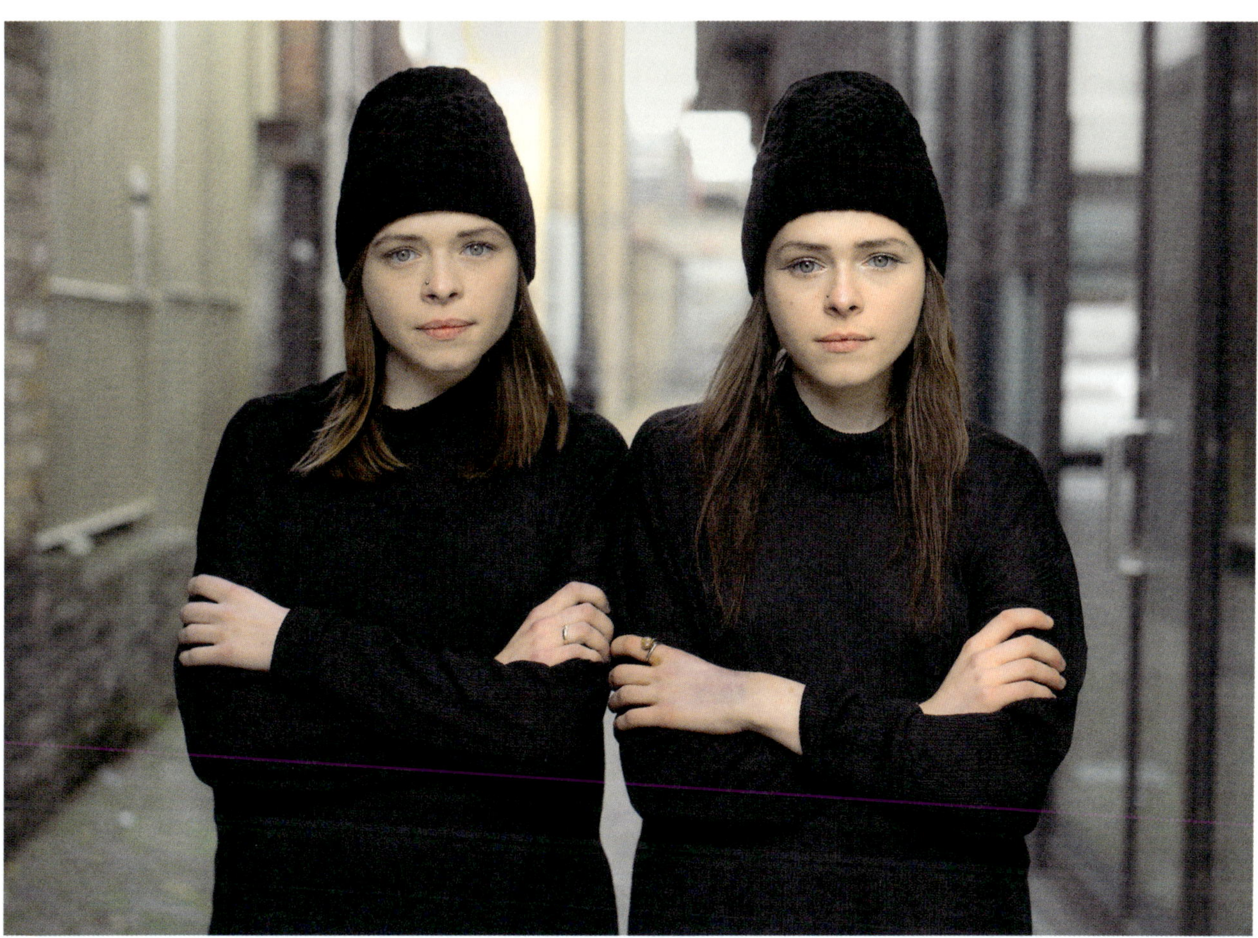

EVA & MARTA

28 years old, Marta older by 2 minutes

'Being twins that work, live and socialise together has its good and bad points. We have
the same vision and passion for our business which might come down to sharing DNA.
Our twinship has made us closer as sisters but it's not something we're obsessed about.
The thought of attending one of those twin conventions makes us cringe.'

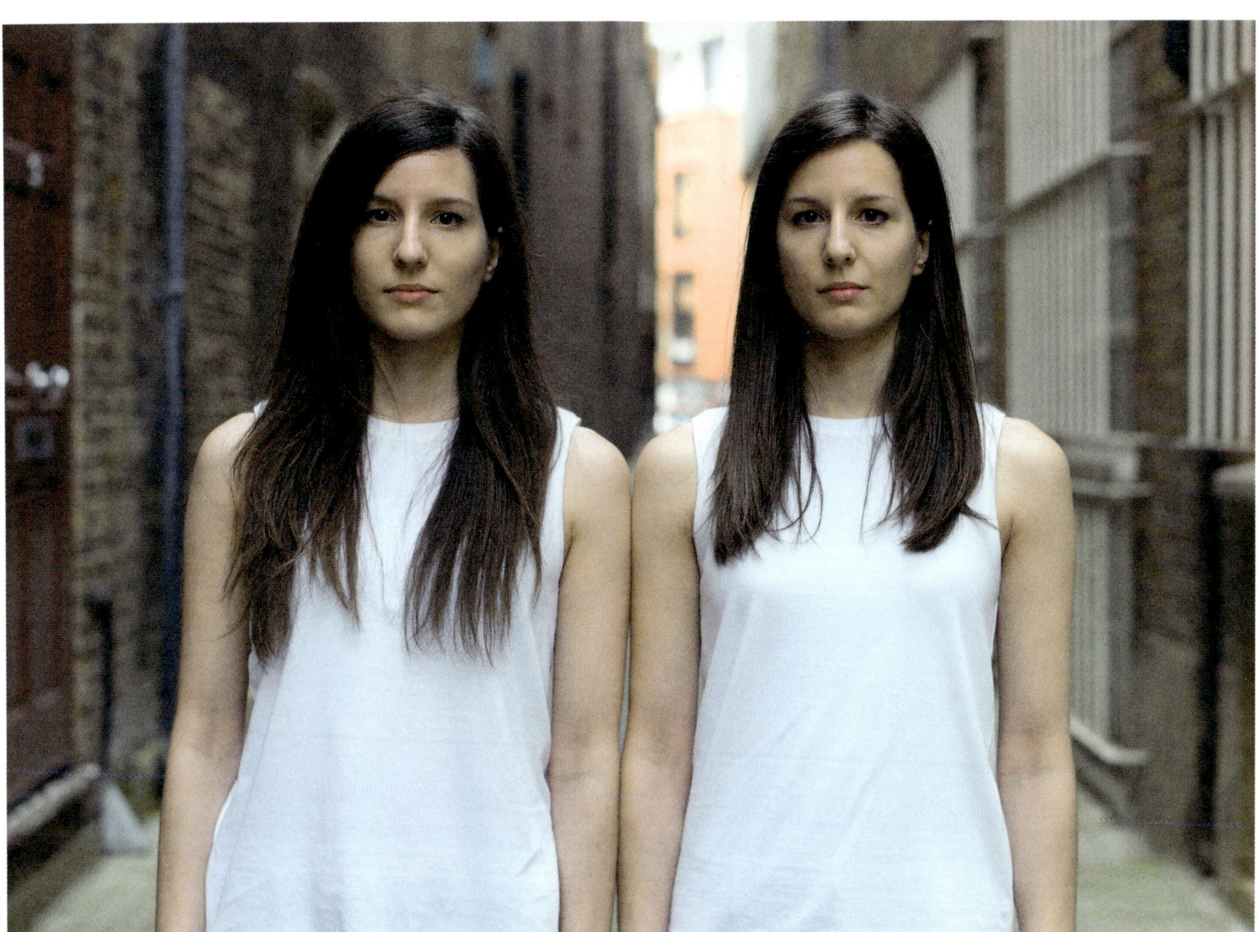

SHARON & IRENE

15 years old, Sharon older by 4 minutes

'We are always there for each other and feel uncomfortable whenever we are separated.
We often say the same things at exactly the same time too.'

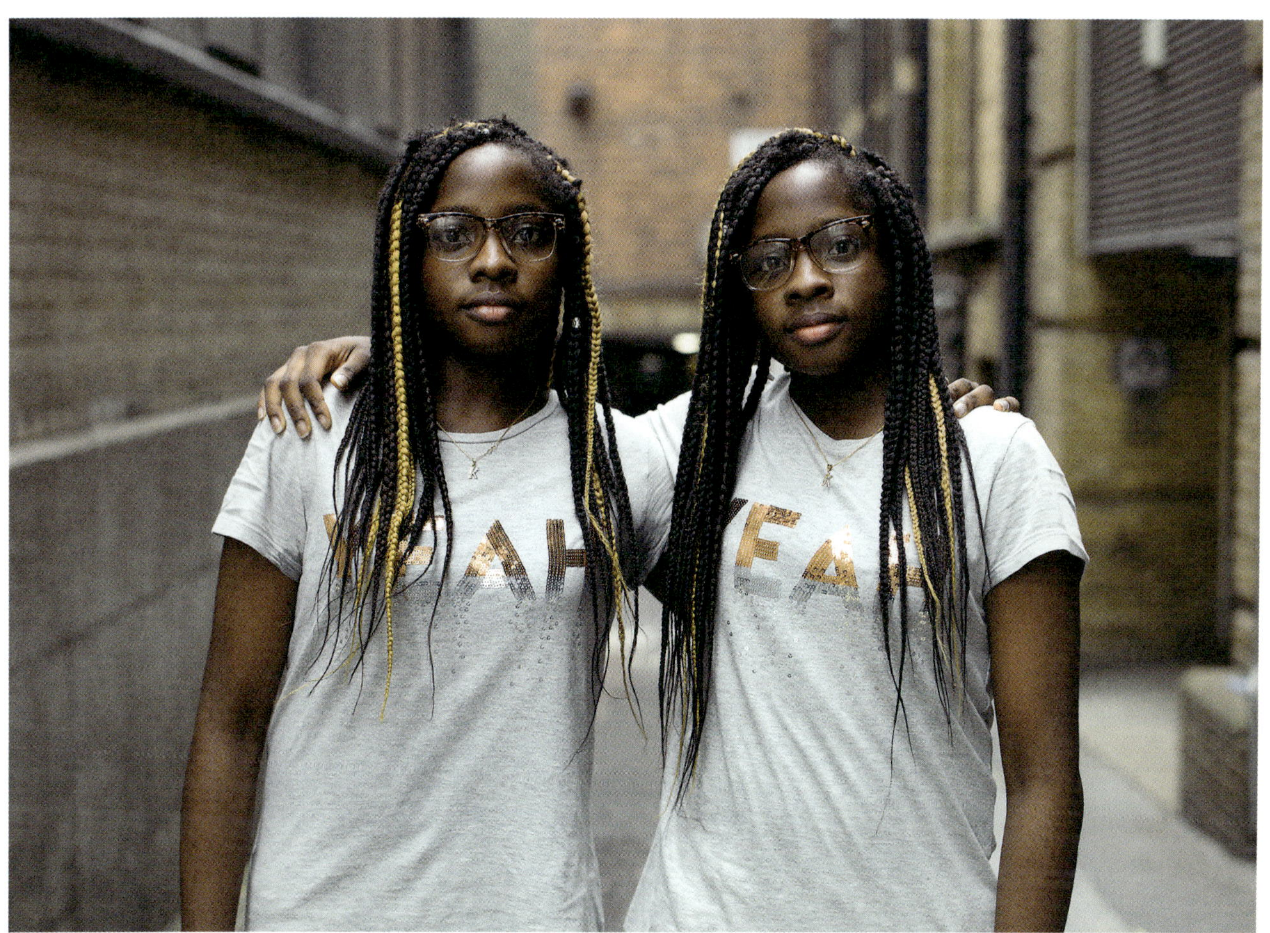

BILL & TOBY

14 years old, Bill older by 3 minutes

'When we were younger we had our picture taken for a magazine and the photographer also included our older brother in the shoot. But, when the magazine was published, we saw that the editor had cropped him out of the photograph, leaving just the two of us. We teased him afterwards saying it was because twins are so special.'

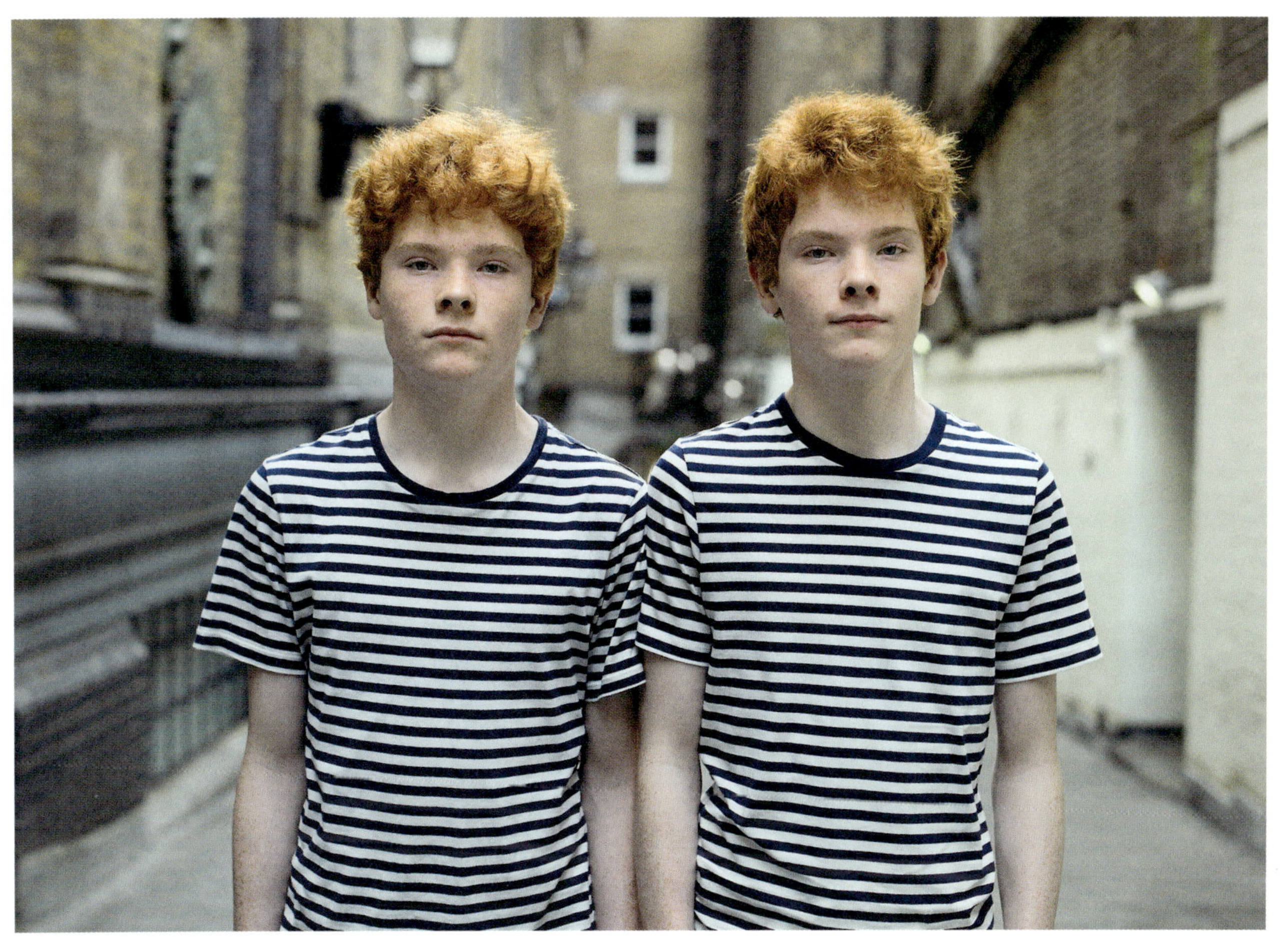

JULIA & SOPHIE

6 years old, Sophie older by 20 minutes

'We are always changing our minds on what we want to be when we grow up. I love art, I am always drawing and would love to be a famous cartoonist one day. Sophie loves animals and dreams of being a gamekeeper. The most important thing to us is making sure we are always first to help others.'

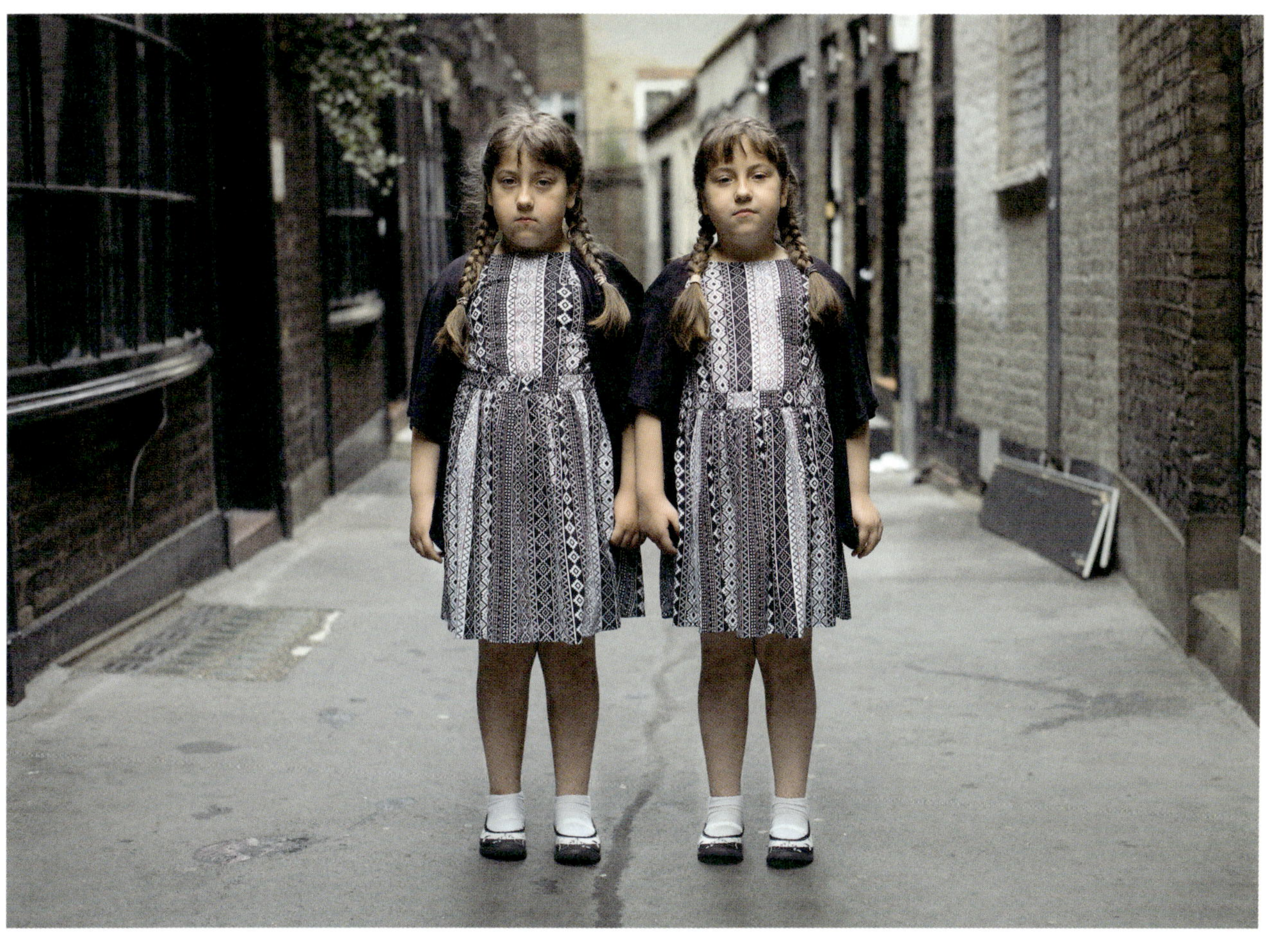

REBECCA & EDWINA

27 years old, Rebecca older by 13 minutes

'During a holiday in Italy I became very ill and was hospitalised. Rebecca came to visit me in the evening but when she was leaving the doctor saw her exiting the hospital and went crazy, shouting in Italian and angrily gesticulating. He didn't realise I had a twin and assumed I was discharging myself! The language barrier prevented Mum from explaining so she had to bring the doctor back to the ward to prove we were twins.'

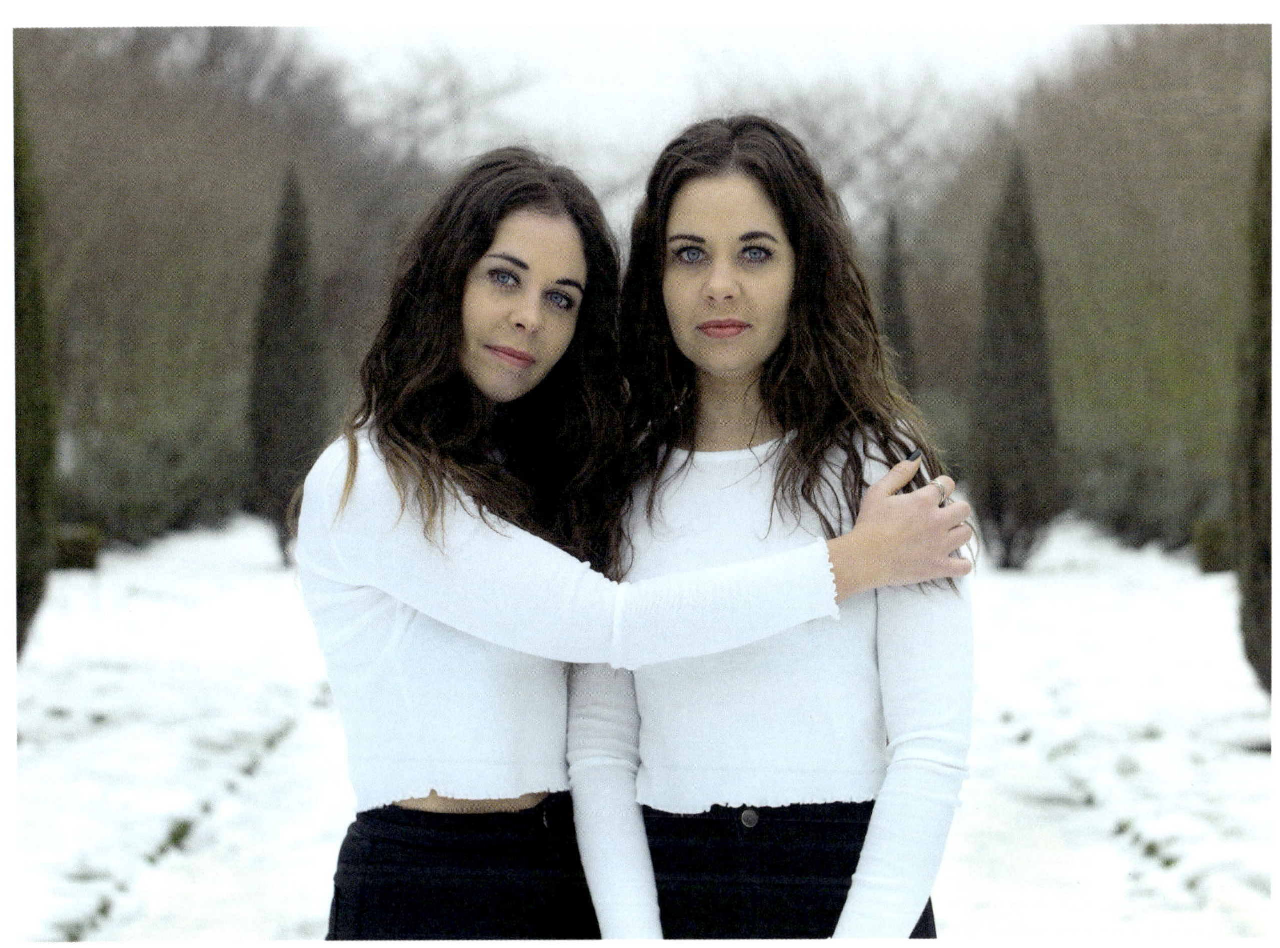

MARIE & KATEŘINA

25 years old, Kateřina older by 1 minute

'We're always contradicting ourselves. We want people to tell us apart yet we don't want them to be able to. We want people to get to know us but we also want them to keep their distance. We stay locked up tight in our own little private world so that no one can ever hurt us.'

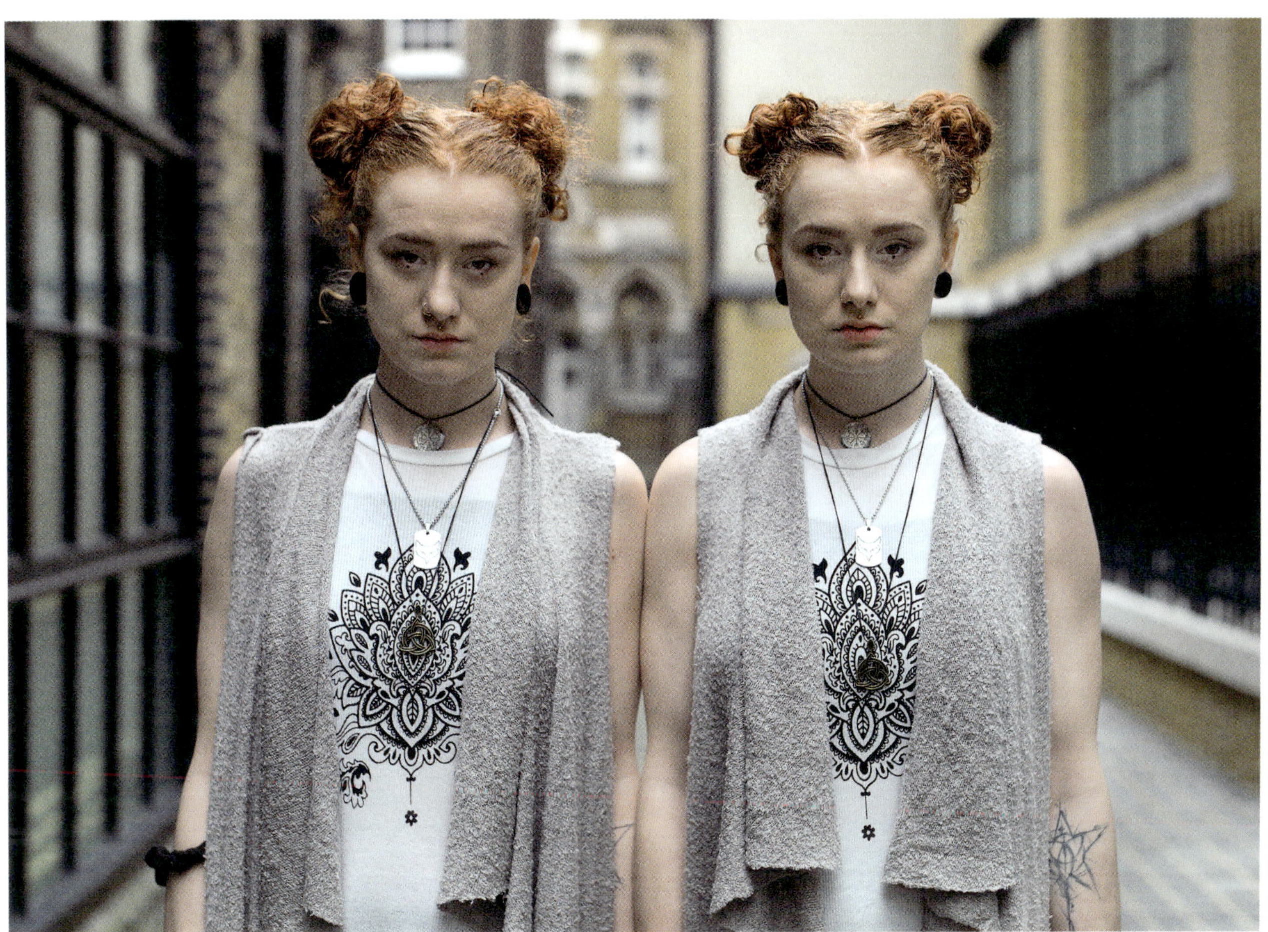

ELSON & ELTON

18 years old, Elson older by 5 minutes

'I first knew I was gay when I was 13. It was a scary feeling but I felt so much better when I talked about it with Elton who told me he was bi-sexual. It was a revelation. We both came out to our parents a few years later and they have been nothing but supportive.'

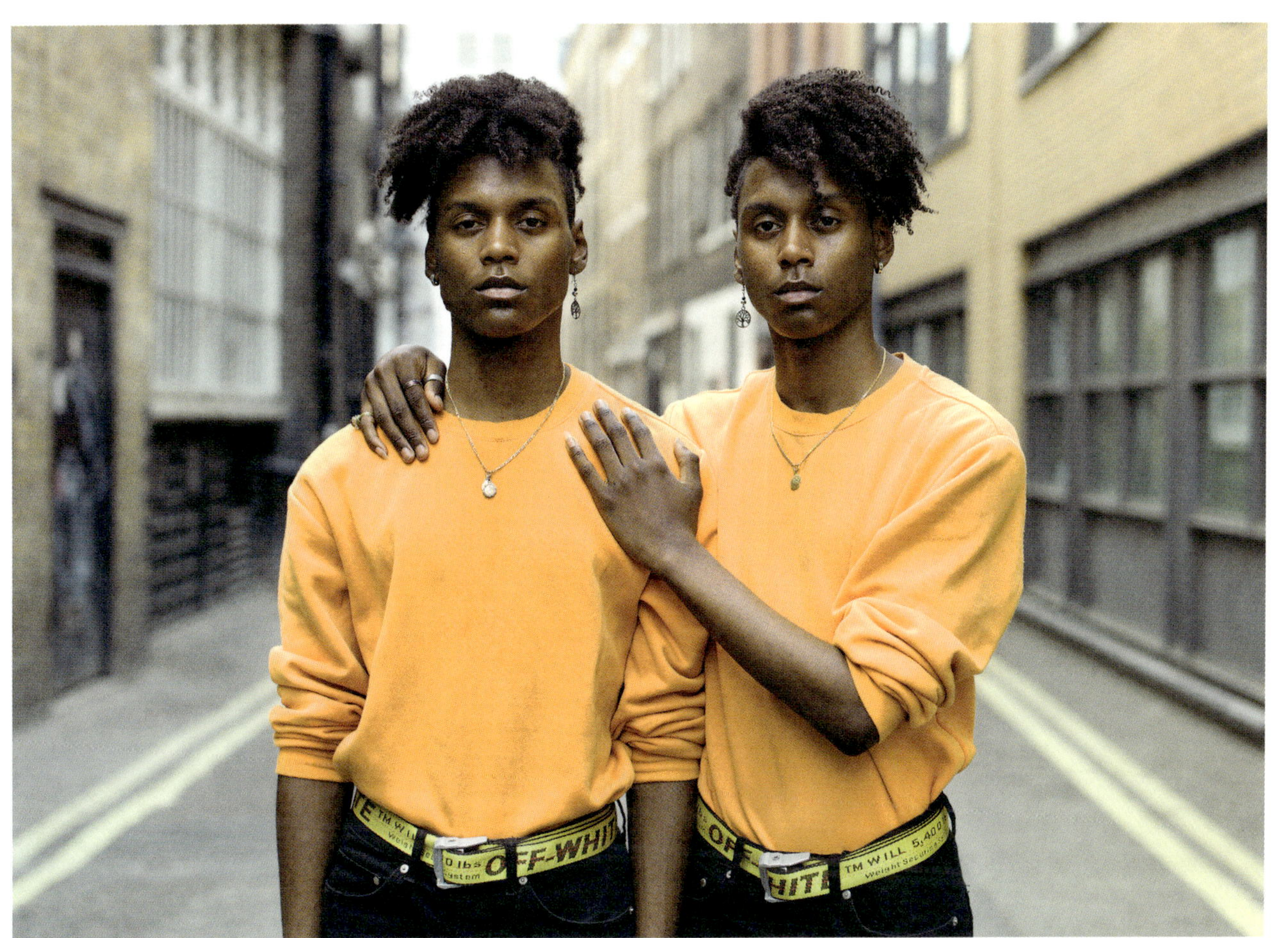

OFF-WHITE
TM WILL 5,400
OFF-WHITE
TM WILL 5,400

AMINE & KARIM

13 years old, Amine older by 1 minute

'We're always playing tricks on people. Our postman had no idea we were twins until one day when we collected the post from him together and he almost had a heart attack.'

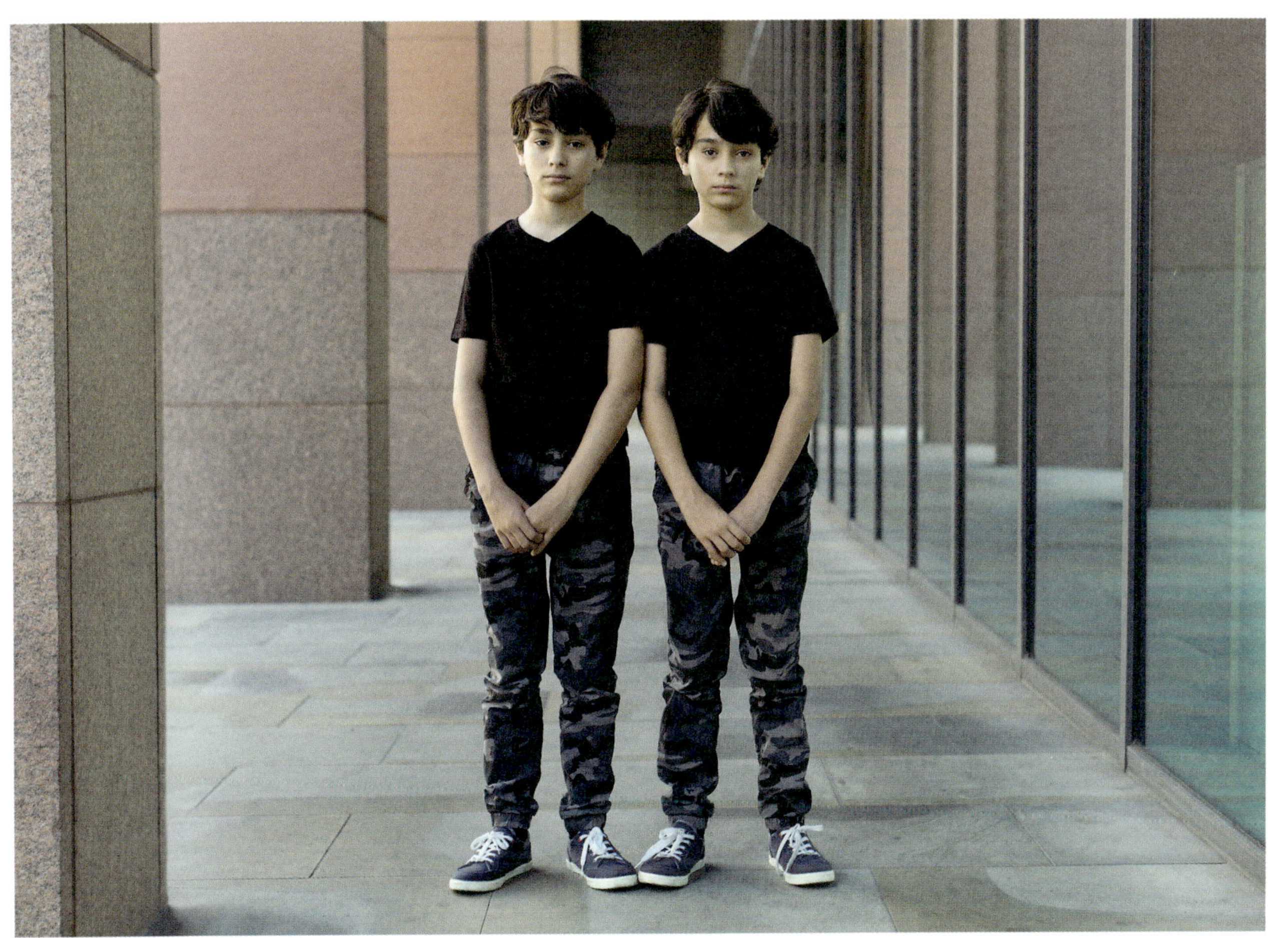

MARIA AND KATIE

36 years old, Katie older by 5 minutes

'At secondary school there was another set of twins who weighed less than us. They were prettier and more popular and we felt insecure. We wanted to be like them. Anorexia has destroyed our lives and we sometimes think we may never recover. We still struggle to make sense of what has happened.'

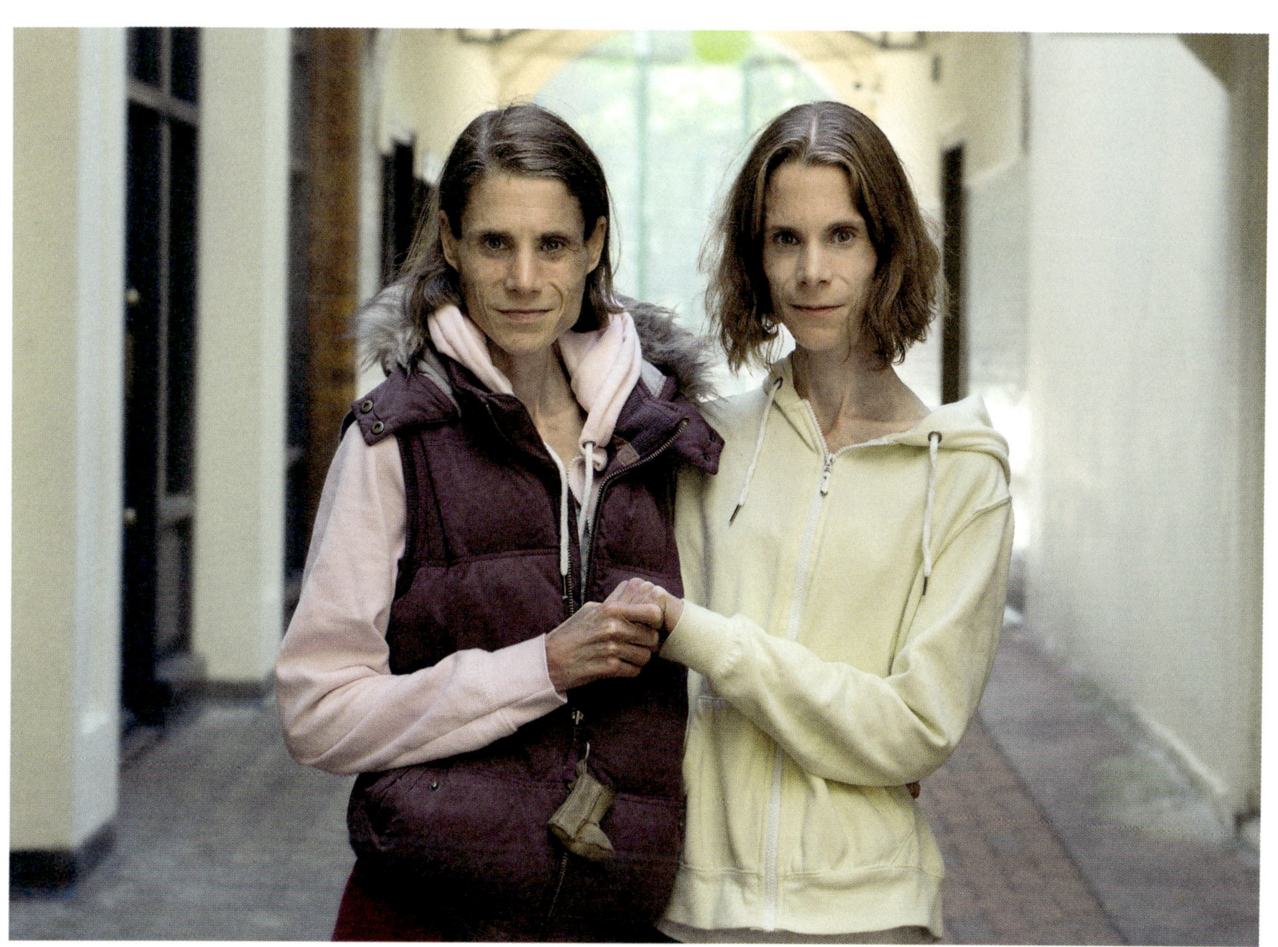

JEREMIE & JOEL

18 years old, Jeremie older by 10 minutes

'When our mum went into labour she thought she was only having one baby because that's what the scan had shown. Shortly after Jeremie was born Mum could tell the pregnancy wasn't over. She got the shock of her life when, 10 minutes later, my little head started to appear.'

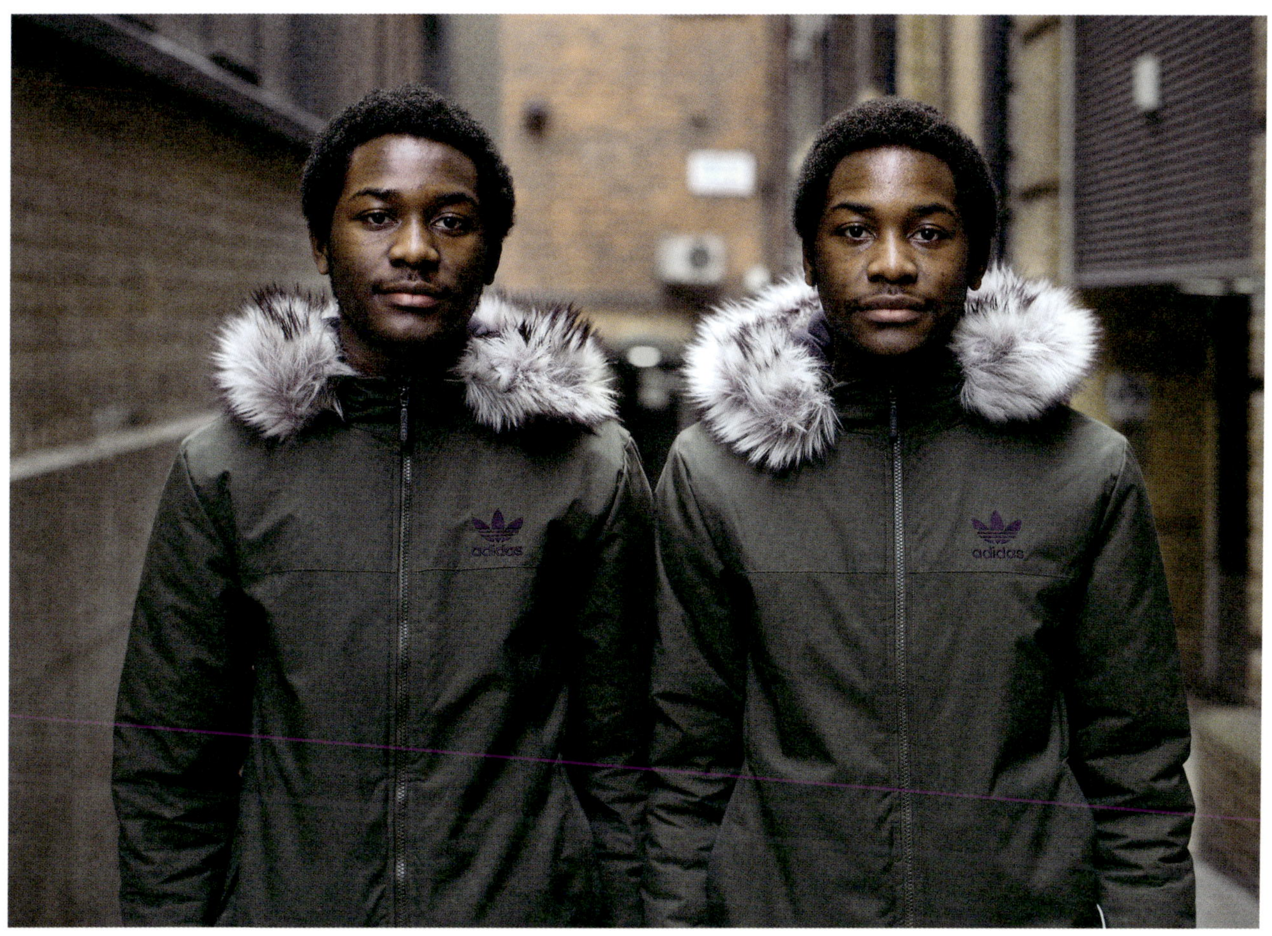

PU & PLA

27 years old, Pu older by 1 minute

'We see ourselves as a unit, our lives count as one. We don't need to speak to be able to
read each other's feelings – we can tell through body language.'

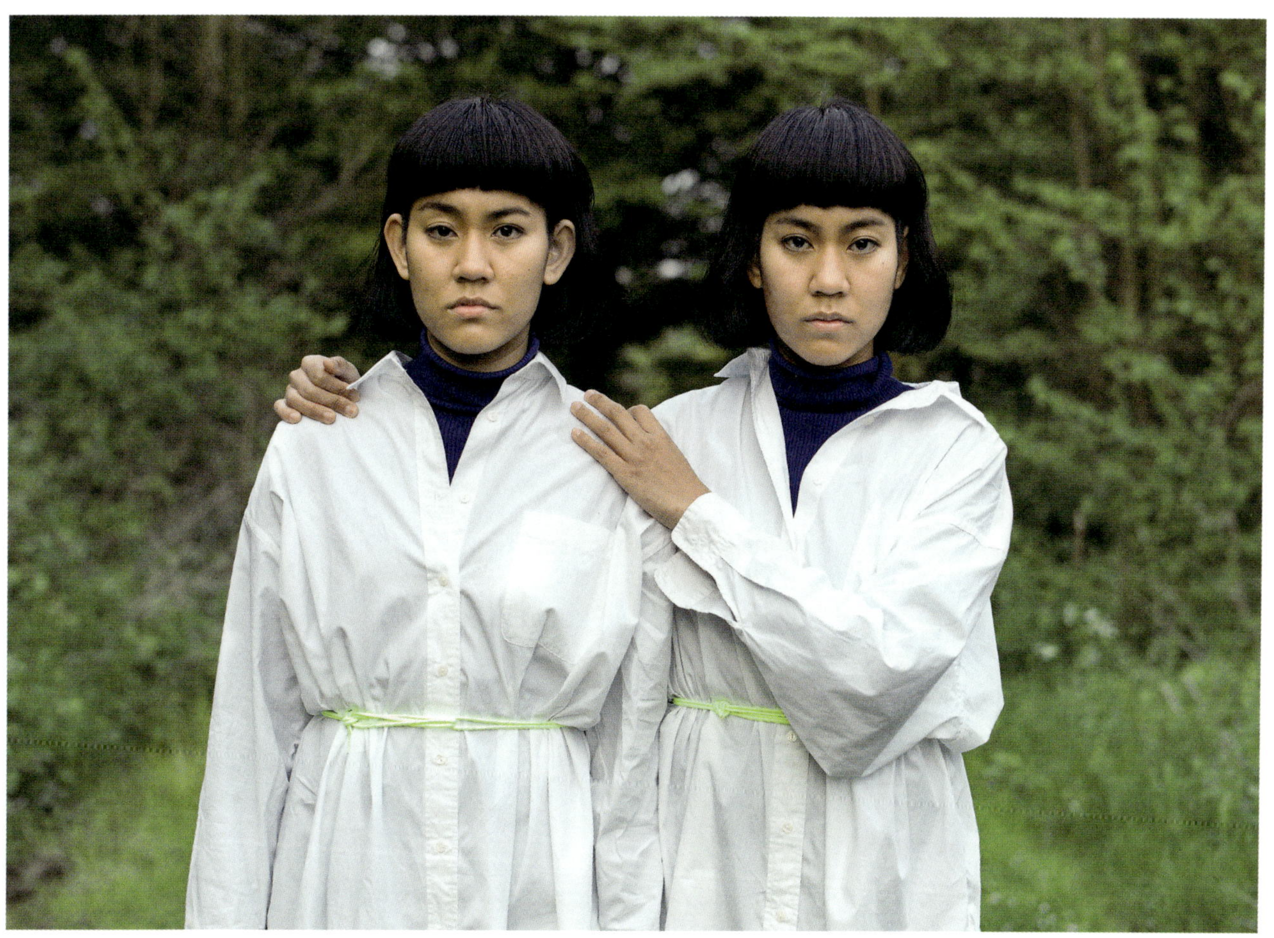

YASMIN & LAILA

6 years old, Yasmin older by 2 minutes

'Everyone is always mixing us up – our friends, our family, even our mum. Sometimes we can't even tell each other apart. Once I thought I was taking a photo of Laila on my phone and I actually had the camera in reverse and I was taking a selfie.'

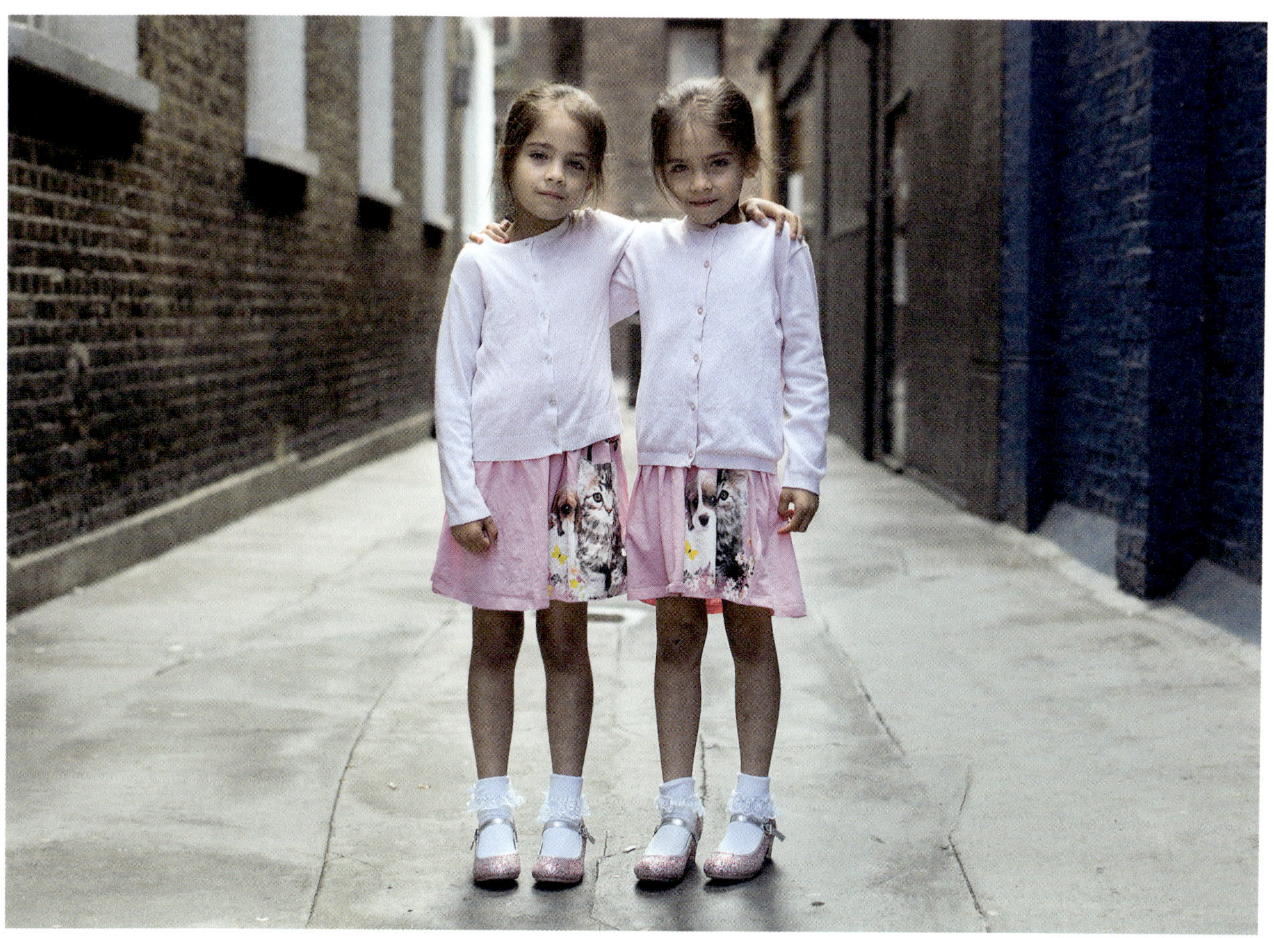

TOMAS & LOURENÇO

15 years old, Tomas older by 1 minute

'Whenever we go on stage we get very nervous but it's easier to be confident when there's two of us. I can't imagine being in a band with anyone else, even though Lourenço always hogs the microphone.'

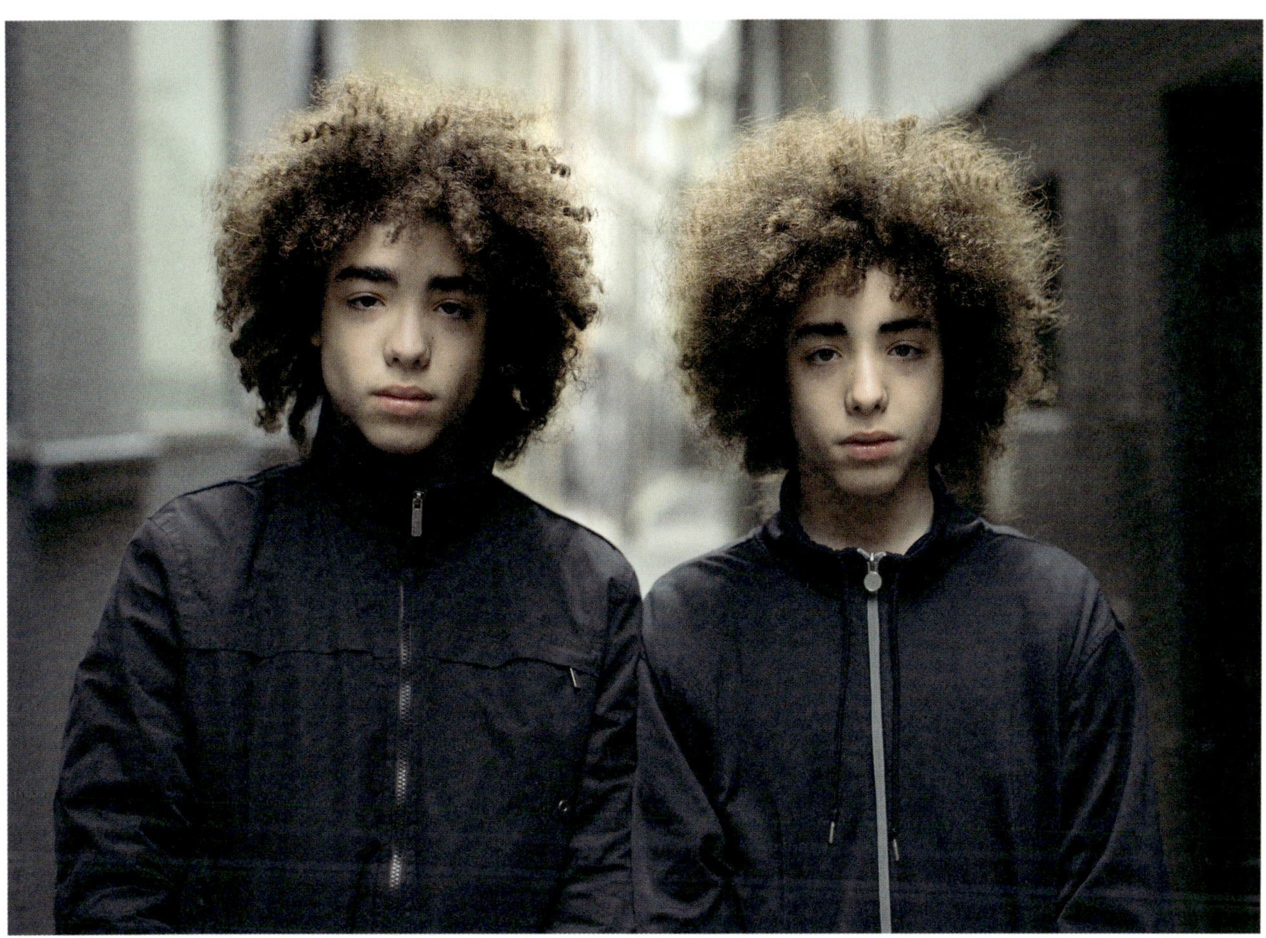

VIOLETA & IRINA

25 years old, Irina older by 1 minute

'It was really important that my parents approved of my new fiancée but equally important that Irina approved of him too. When I marry this will be the first time we will be properly apart. It will be a very weird transition.'

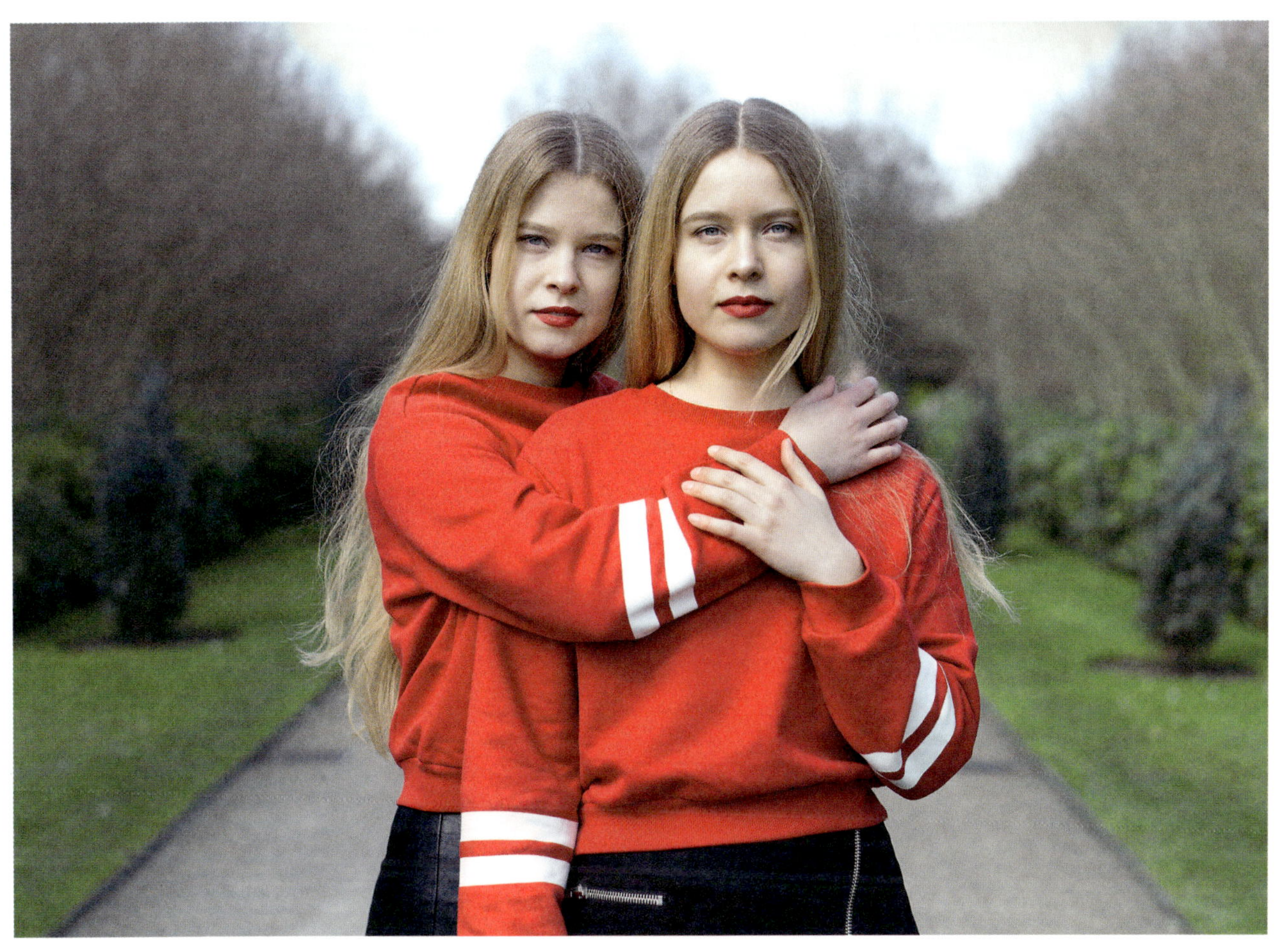

AVEAH & ANAIAH

3 years old, Aveah older by 7 minutes

'As the parents of Aveah and Anaiah, the girls constantly team up and try to run rings around us. We usually dress them in the same outfits because it's one less thing for them to squabble about. It makes life easy for us to buy two of everything. They can learn how to share later.'

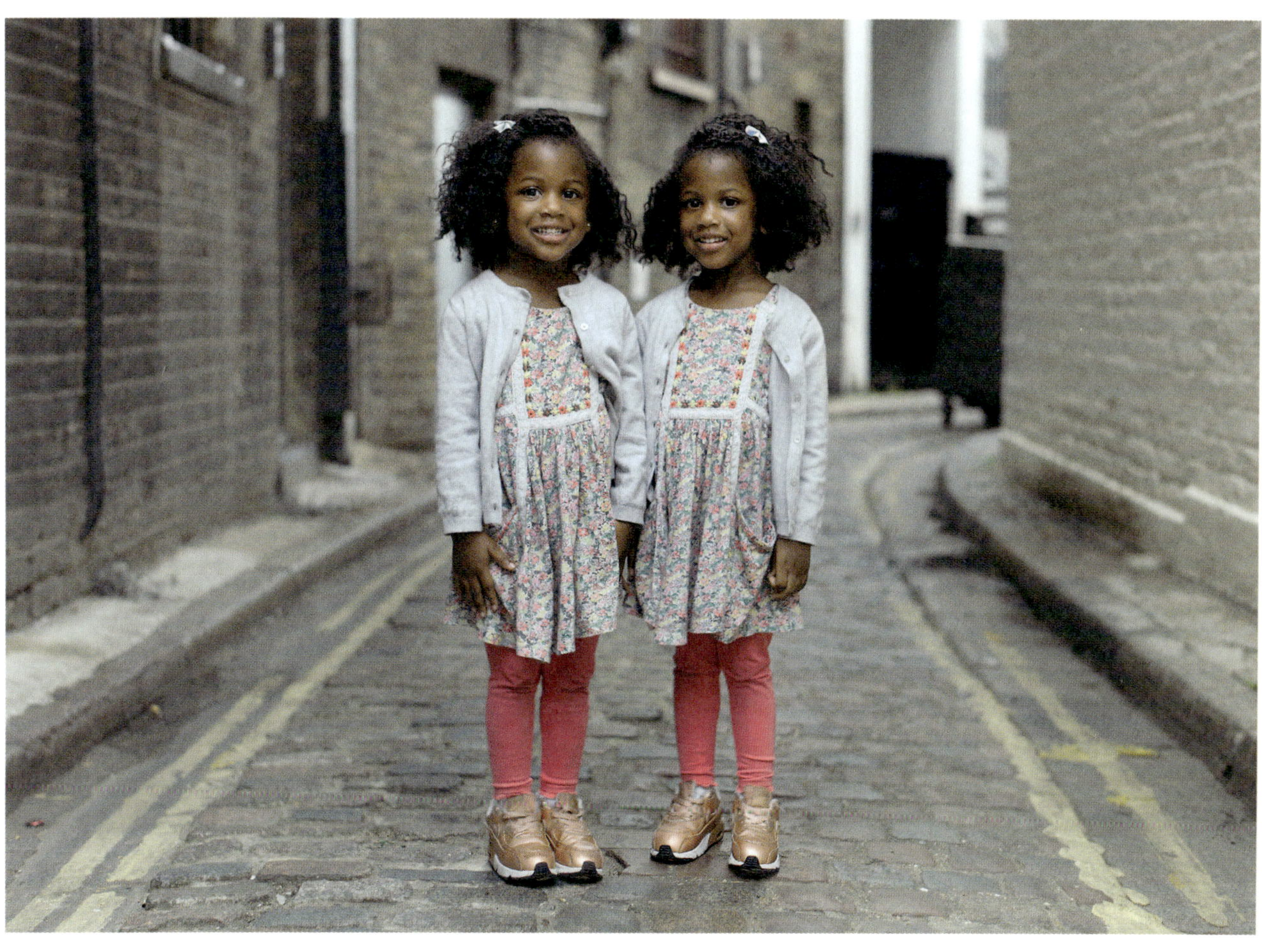

VÅR & RONJA

22 years old, Ronja older by 3 minutes

'Not having each other is something we don't like to think about. That's just too scary. Only by being a twin will you be able to understand the close relationship we share. We are soulmates, best friends and love each other more than anyone else.'

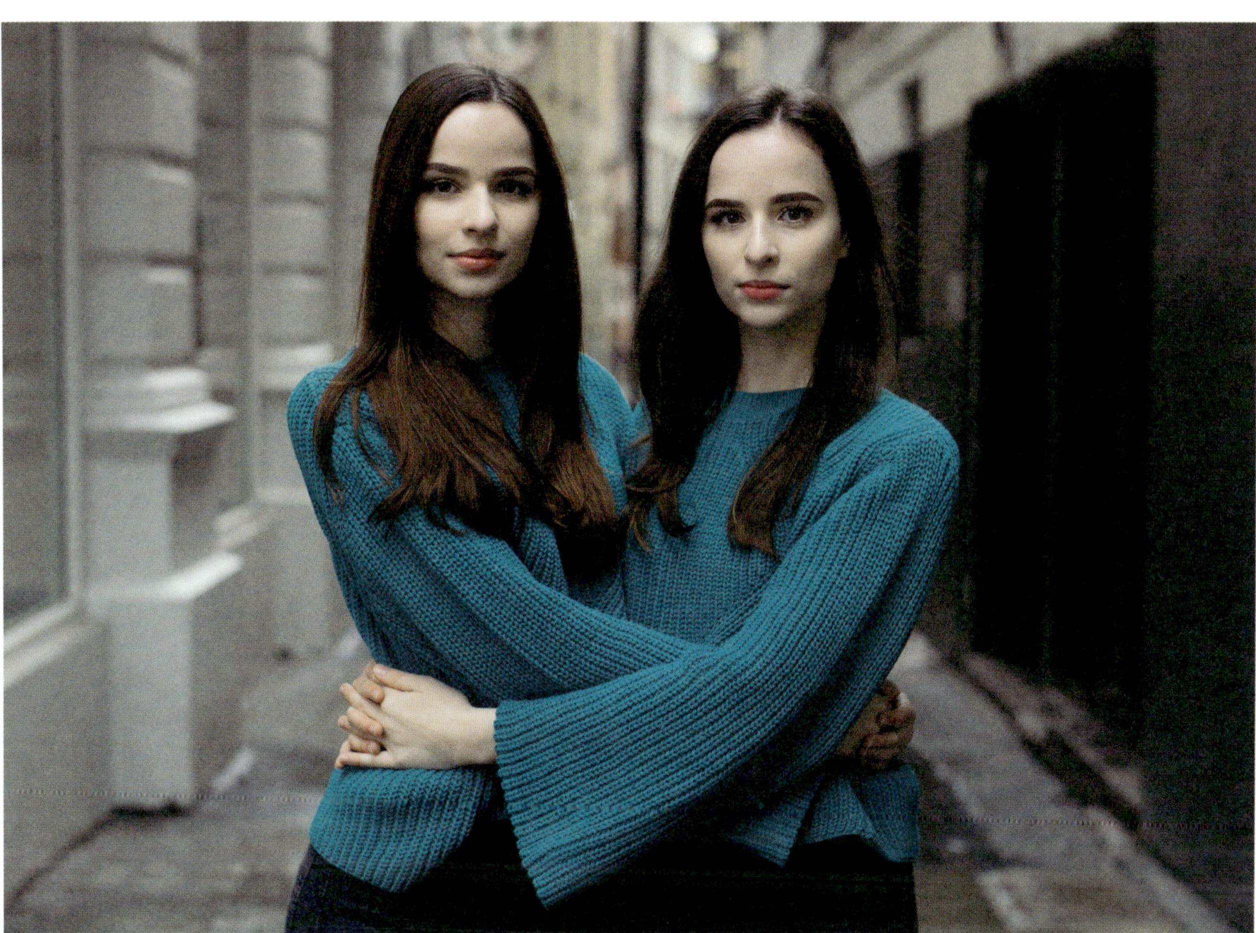

ZACK & NATHAN

16 years old, Zack older by 8 seconds

'It's hard because everyone compares you constantly. We don't like to look alike so we rarely wear the same clothes and don't normally have the same haircut. People still mix us up all the time though – we're used to it.'

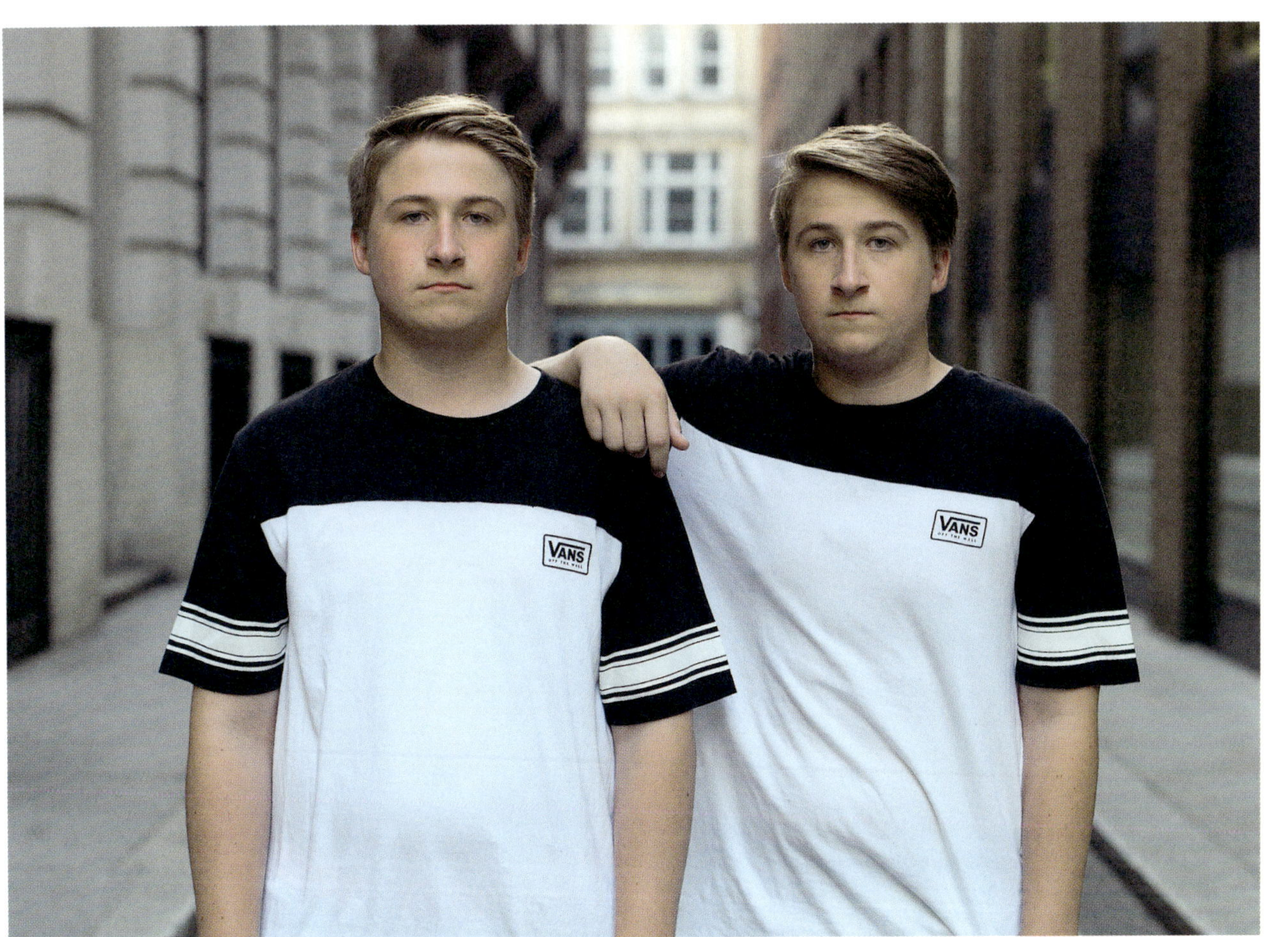

SAMANTHA AND CASILDA

19 years old, Samantha older by 30 minutes

'We both love all types of food – Indian, Chinese, Mexican, whatever. We have almost identical taste buds, except when it comes to peas. Casilda hates peas and picks them out of her Chinese food. I love them. I suppose we can't agree on everything.'

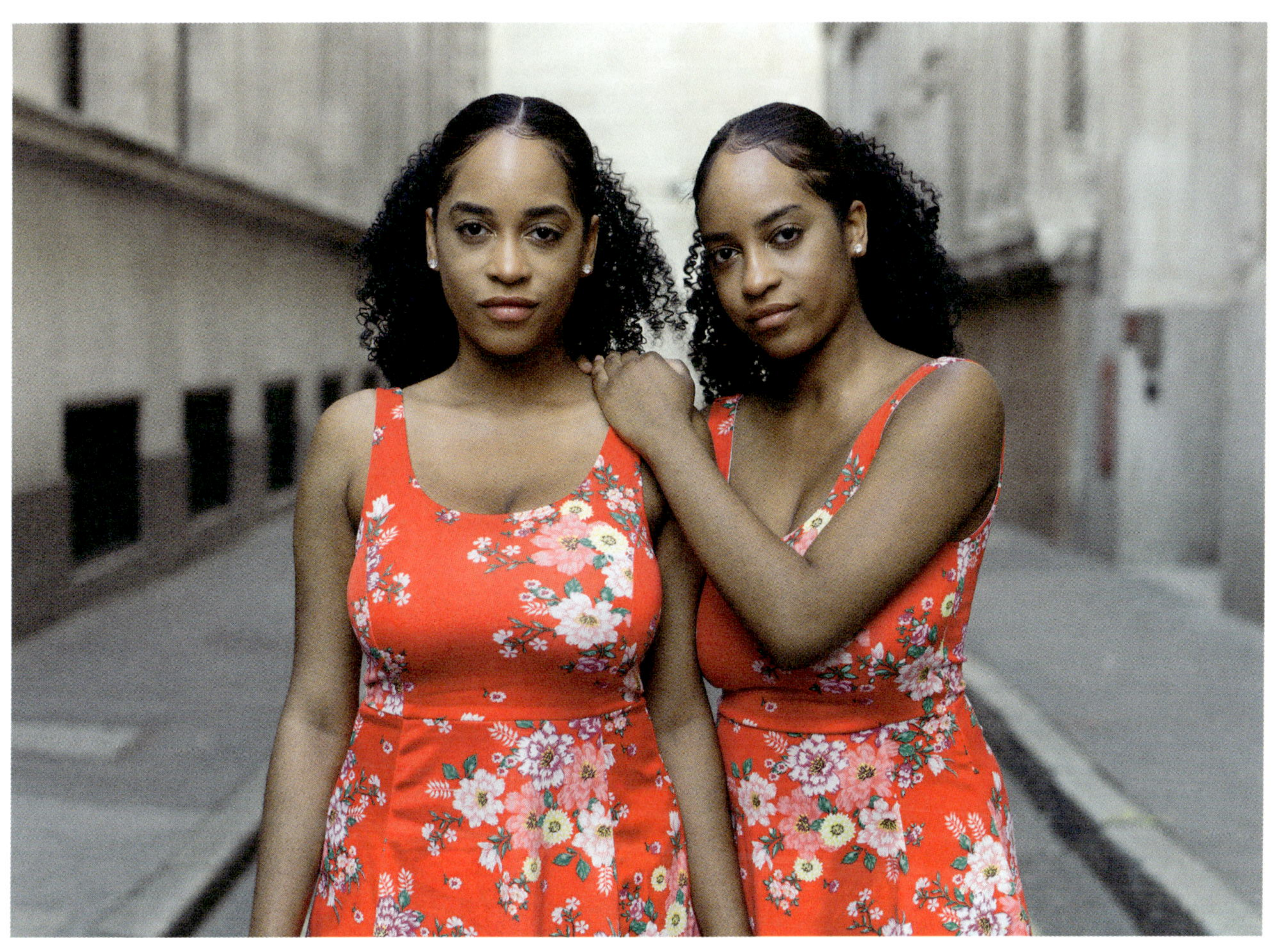

GRACE & SOPHIA

6 years old, Grace older by 1 minute

'We may look the same but we have different feelings. Our favourite quote is by Walt Disney who said, "If you can dream it, you can do it." I love my sister.'

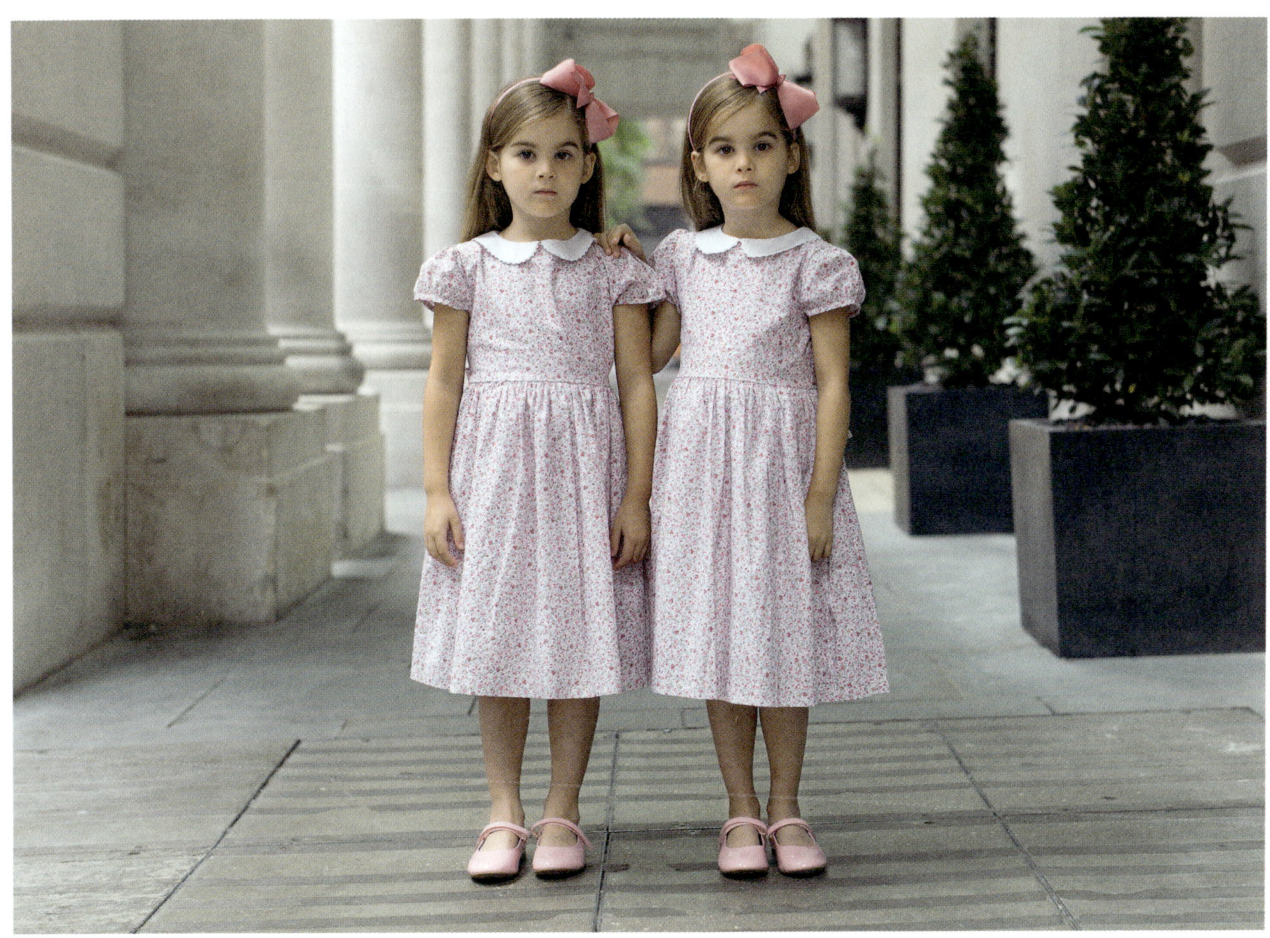

NAOMI & ALEXANDRIA

30 years old, Naomi older by 30 minutes

'Growing up we felt being a twin was a curse. People referred to us as "the twins" and we struggled to develop individual identities. We tried hard to be different from each other, choosing certain colours that the other was banned from wearing. Now, being a twin is a huge part of who we are. We live apart and have our own lives but we still do most things together and talk every day.'

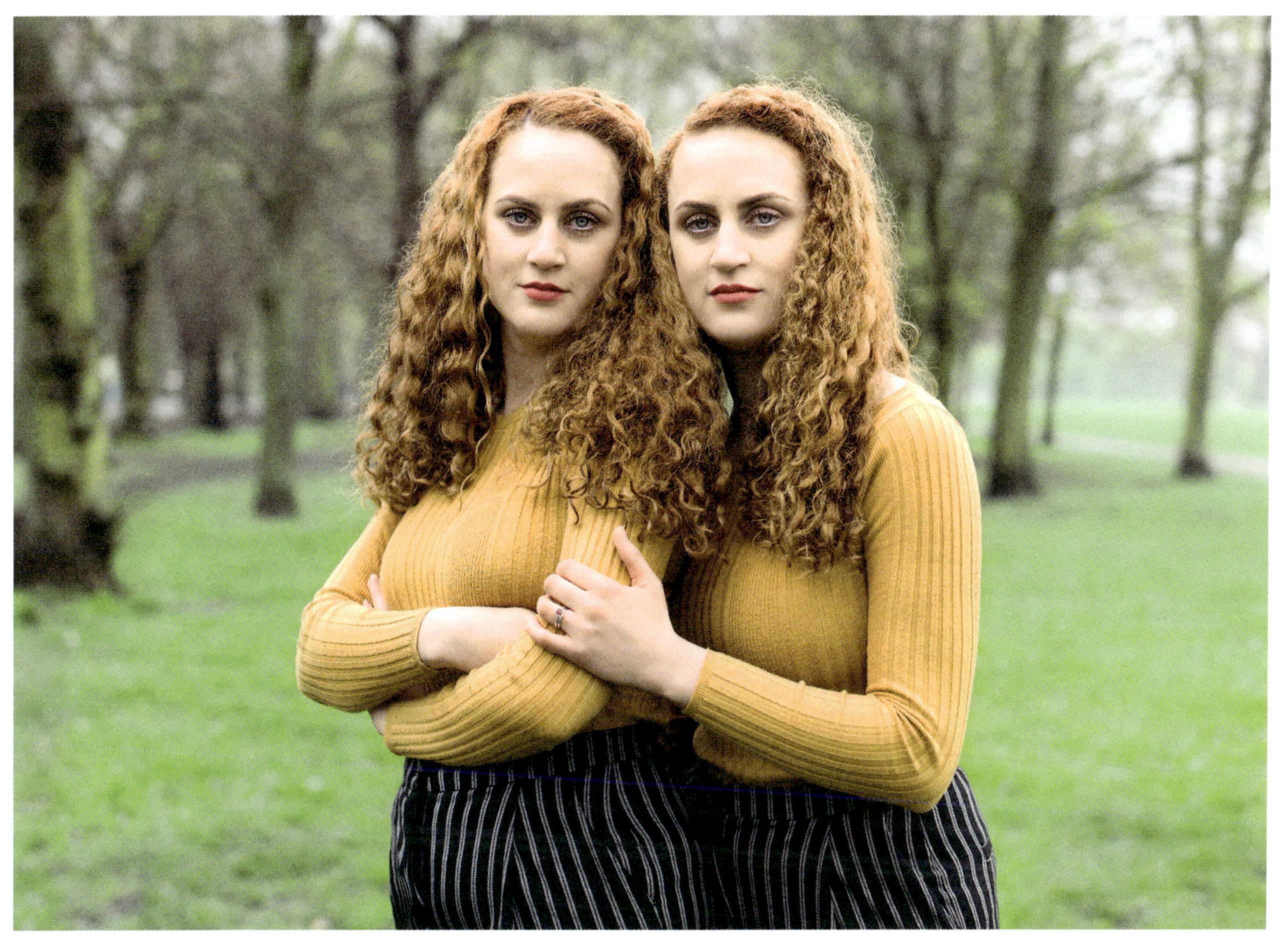